BEACHCRAFT BONANZA

written and illustrated by

Brian J. Heinz

Foreword by Les Paldy, Director of the Center for Science, Mathematics and Technology Education, State University of New York at Stony Brook

Published by

BALLyhoo BOOKS

P.O. Box 534
Shoreham, NY 11786

4/26/86
Eileen ~
May the book be of lasting value.
Enjoy.
Love!
Brian

BEACHCRAFT BONANZA

First printing: January, 1986

ISBN: 0-936335-00-9

Library of Congress Cataloging-in-Publication Data

Heinz, Brian, 1946-
    Beachcraft bonanza.

    Bibliography: p.
    Summary: Suggest craft and art activities and nature study experiments for the Atlantic seashore, including seaweed mounting, a marine aquarium, seashell planters, gull feather pens, and starfish Santas.
    1. Beaches--Atlantic Coast (U.S.)--Study and teaching (Secondary) 2. Coasts--Atlantic Coast (U.S.)--Study and teaching (Secondary) 3. Marine biology--Atlantic Coast (U.S.)--Study and teaching (Secondary) 4. Nature craft--Study and teaching (Secondary) [1. Seashore biology. 2. Nature craft. 3. Handicraft] I. Title.

GB459.4.H44 1986   508 .314'6   86-2272
ISBN 0-936335-00-9 (pbk.)

Printed in the United States of America

For my family and friends...

And for all my students...

Past, present, and future...

ACKNOWLEDGEMENTS

No book is ever solely the work of an individual. The words are born of experiences and ideas encountered and shared among many people and in many places. The following are but a few who contributed greatly in giving these ideas substance,…in making this book a reality.

Ann Brassard — for instructing the author in illustrating and preparing mechanicals.

Marty Ferris — for the Ballyhoo Books imprint in Celtic calligraphy.

Don Ferruzzi of Biomateria Publishing — for pre-press assistance.

Gwen — for the interminable loan of a typewriter.

Dale Hodges, librarian extraordinaire — for words of encouragement and honest critiques.

Shelley Lantheaume of Camera Ready Typesetters — for her time, advice, and assistance in preparing the manuscript galleys.

Lou and Dan Presutti of East Coast Graphics — for patience, guidance, and dedication to excellence.

Jim Slattery — for the photography of finished crafts.

Ray Sevin of Bookmasters — for availability and quick responses to questions and concerns.

My Students — for successfully proving the value of the ideas in this book.

CONTENTS

FOREWORD

Brian Heinz's *Beachcraft Bonanza* is a superb guide featuring science, nature study and art activities at the seashore. It is a fine supplement to standard field guides for persons who live near the northeastern beaches and tidal zones of the U.S. The activities in the guide can be used by teachers, parents and others who are responsible for organizing shore outings. The activities are simple and can be carried out by persons of nearly all ages. They will provide knowledge and enjoyment to those who try them.

Users of the guide will also become more aware of the diversity of the organisms and environments that can be found at our beaches and estuaries. The author's respect for the environment and his knowledge of the systems he describes illuminate the book and make it attractive to read.

The activities can be performed with materials found at the beach, or require only the most commonly available household items. Everyone will be able to succeed with these activities, which do not require great manual dexterity, or prior knowledge and scientific or artistic training. Most of the activities do not require a great deal of time to perform. Even small children with limited attention spans will find things to do here.

Science, art, a sense of accomplishment and sheer fun all await readers of Brian's book. Try some of the activities and see for yourself how easy and interesting they are.

Les Paldy, Director

Center for Science, Mathematics and Technology Education,
State University of New York at Stony Brook

AUTHOR'S NOTE

The sea has always drawn people to its shores. Those that come inevitably display an unbounded curiosity for the landscapes and oddities of life that flourish there. It is hoped that this simple text will be seen as more than just a collection of crafts and activities. It is designed to help readers discover the natural beauty within the unique environments and eco-systems of our ocean beaches through a wide variety of hands-on activities which include arts, crafts, experiments, puzzles, scavenger hunts, and collection devices.

Our Atlantic coastal environment has always played an important role in our history and in our social and cultural development. Each unit has been gently infused with facts relating to these themes, and with ideas that provide a basic understanding of the delicate and important relationships that exist between man and the beach, and the dynamics within the coastal eco-system itself.

This book may be a springboard to more technical texts as suggested in the bibliography, but mostly the book should be fun. The activities are non-threatening. They have been successfully accomplished and proven valuable by seven-year-old elementary school students and senior citizens alike.

Enjoy the book. Enjoy the beach.

Brian Heinz

CLAMSHELL SCRIMSHAW

Avast, ye lubbers, and listen well! Here's an idea to stiffen your jib as we drift back into marine history....

Scrimshaw is the ancient seafarer's art of carving intricate line drawings into whale ivory, much of it coming from the teeth and jawbone of the sperm whale. Lampblack was then rubbed into the scratches to accentuate the drawings and the ivory surface was polished.

Whaleship voyages of three years and longer were common during the 1800's. The art of scrimshaw (also called scrimshander) provided seamen with hours of pleasant diversion from the toiling labors of whaling.

Whaling and all whale products are now outlawed in the United States, but you can create a beautiful seascape on a natural substitute for whale ivory — the clam shell!

Let's heave anchor, mate, and get underway.

At the beach, collect large surf clam shells which are often six to eight inches wide. The best time to look is in the spring or fall when human traffic on the beach is light. But, if you can't find suitable shells, a seafood restaurant will happily donate some steamer clam shells (if you don't mind the odd looks your request is sure to bring).

Next, wash the shells, inside and out, and dry them.

Sailors etched their designs with sailmakers' needles, but you will not need any sharp metal carving tools. Instead, your tools will be a sharp pencil and a black permanent marker pen (felt or porous tip) with an ultra-fine point. They are inexpensive and can be bought at any stationery.

Plan your scene on paper first....A spouting whale?...A ship at sea?...A mermaid or a sea serpent?

When you are satisfied with your drawing, select a shell half of good quality. Use the pencil to lightly transfer your scene to the *inside* surface of the clam shell. Keep your pencil sharp. Any error can be easily erased.

With your pencil sketch satisfactorily completed on the shell, *slowly* and *carefully* retrace your scene with the black marker pen. Remember you are working on a hard slippery surface. (Ultra-fine markers are available in colors if you wish to highlight your artwork.)

To preserve your "scrimshaw," spray lightly with clear shellac or art "fixative." These products are available at art, hobby, or hardware stores.

Your clamshell scrimshaw can be glued (white glue) onto plain wooden bookends or plaques; they can be used as paperweights or can be mounted on a wire stand to be displayed proudly on a shelf or mantel.

Aye, me hearties! Now there's a sight to melt your barnacles!

Clamshell Scrimshaw

Clamshell Art by Shannon Delgado, age 9

If you're interested in seeing true scrimshaw art, check your local museums. Some jewelers, antique dealers, and art galleries are licensed to deal in scrimshaw, also.

If you wish to try your hand at authentic scrimshaw art, a starter kit can be purchased from:

> Port of Ivory
> 126 Main Street
> Port Jefferson, NY 11777
> (516) 928-5434

The kit contains a steel scribe, India ink, a practice piece of polymer, an actual chip of whale ivory, and complete instructions. Call and ask for Bernard Boriosi, the resident scrimshaw artist and proprietor. He'll be glad to help you. Better yet, visit this unique nautical shop of brass, shell, and ivory collectibles and jewelry. You'll also see magnificent examples of scrimshander art.

Clamshell Scrimshaw by the author

MAGIC DANCING SAND

So,...you think geology is boring? Wrong! Here's a great way to have some fun and learn a little about beach geology at the same time.

Tape a thin sheet of white paper onto an old picture frame, 5 inches by 7 inches or larger. Neatly trim the paper to size along the border of the frame and be sure the paper is taut from edge to edge. (See illustration.)

You will need a magnet. A bar magnet works best, but any small strong magnet will do. If you are using a small square magnet or disc magnet, attach it with cellophane tape to the end of a dowel or stick. That was easy enough. Right?

Now, for the real fun!

At the base of the dunes on an ocean beach, you will usually notice strands of sand with a purplish hue. (This sand provides the best results but any sand will work, even from your own backyard.)

Be sure the sand is dry. Scoop a small amount into your hand and sprinkle a very thin layer over your paper frame. Grasp the edge of the frame securely and hold it level. Place your magnet *under* the paper, touching the paper lightly, and gently move the magnet back and forth and in circular motions.

WOW! Dancing sand!

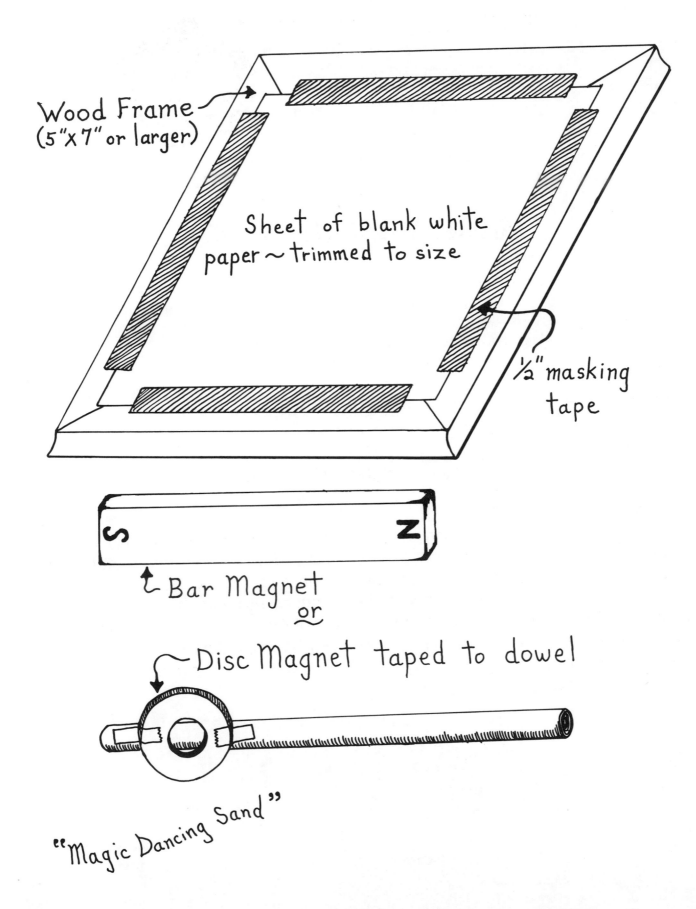

Wood Frame
(5"x 7" or larger)

Sheet of blank white
paper ~ trimmed to size

½" masking
tape

S   N

↑ Bar Magnet
or

Disc Magnet taped to dowel

"Magic Dancing Sand"

Why Does it Work?

Beach sand (especially the purplish sand at the base of dunes) is made up mostly of yellowish white grains of quartz (silicon dioxide). It also contains grains of red garnet (a hard gemstone used in fine sandpapers), pinkish grains of feldspar, and black grains of a mineral called magnetite. It is the magnetite which is attracted to your magnet, an obvious reason for its name.

The grains of garnet and magnetite are heavier than the particles of silicon. They are thrown up onto the dunes by powerful storm waves but, as the waves have spent most of their energy pounding the dune, the receding water is too weak to drag these heavier particles back to the sea. And so they are deposited at the base of the dunes. It is the mixture of black magnetite, red garnet, and yellowish quartz that gives this sand its purplish color.

With a magnifying glass you can easily identify each grain and see the true colors. Magnify them in the sunlight. They look like little jewels! If you have a "good eye" you will even find tiny fragments of sea shells that have become part of the "sand."

Start a Mineral Collection

You can separate enough magnetite from the sand to fill a small bottle. Label it with the date and location and start a mineral collection. Try not to get the magnetite directly on your magnet. It is almost impossible to get off. Separate it out by using your frame. Hold the magnet against the paper from below. Now, tilt the frame and allow the sand to pour off. The magnetite will remain, held by your magnet. Remove the magnet and tap the loose grains of magnetite into your collection bottle. (Medicine vials work beautifully and are available at your drugstore. Just ask the pharmacist.)

Repeat the collection procedure until you have the amount you need.

Now, go out and amaze your friends!

You can purchase powerful disc magnets and hand lenses from:

MUSEUM PRODUCTS
3175 Gold Star Highway
Mystic, CT 06355
Telephone: (203) 536-6433

The company carries a wide variety of products related to nature and science. Their products are inexpensive, yet they are of good quality. Call or write for their free catalog.

MINI-DUNE COLLAGE

We've all experienced the sadness that overcomes us when it's time to leave the beach. Well, now you can take a piece of the beach home with you, to look at and touch, to re-experience the peace and beauty of the shore.

Your materials are simple and readily available:

- 2 or 3 cans of assorted spray paints (Try for at least one warm and one cool color. Red, orange and yellow are "warm" colors. Blue, green, and violet are "cool" colors.)
- A piece of shirt cardboard or heavy oaktag (6" x 12" or larger; any color will do)
- bottle of white glue and a small paint brush
- black fine-tip marker or felt pen and a pencil
- beach sand
- assorted beach debris (driftwood twigs, shells or shell fragments, plant sprigs and dried grasses, pebbles, rope, feathers, crab claws or bones collected at the shore.)

This craft can be done right on the beach. A small bag will hold your paint, glue, pens, and cardboard while you walk along the high tide line. Here you will see long thin mounds of beach debris washed ashore by the tides and waves. Finger through the dried seaweed for interesting items to be glued later to your collage.

Preparing the Background

With your materials assembled, your first task is to spray a colorful background onto your cardboard.

Lay the cardboard lengthwise and flat on the sand in front of you. Be sure your back is to the wind so the paint spray will be carried away from you. And be sure no other people are nearby to be disturbed by your work.

Hold the spray can about ten inches from the cardboard and *lightly dust* a few small sections on the upper half. This will become the sky on your scene. Do *not* spray continuously, as the paint will run down in streaky drips. A few short bursts of color will do nicely. You are not trying to paint the entire surface of the cardboard. You are adding only highlights of color.

Now spray a few bursts of a contrasting color or, if you wish, a complementary color. Each blend of colors will create a different and distinctive "mood" to your work. A sky of blues and greens might give a sense of tranquility or loneliness. Reds and yellows might shout happiness or excitement. For a mood of power, try violet and red or yellow.

Allow the paint to dry for a few moments.

Next, take your pencil and draw a continuous line of rolling dunes from side edge to side edge of your cardboard. Your dune line should begin about 1/3 of the way up from the bottom edge of the cardboard.

Take the paintbrush and liberally coat the entire area below the dune line with white glue. (You can spread it with your finger, also.) Be sure the glue has a neat continuous flow along your dune line. With this done, sprinkle handfuls of sand onto the glue. Use plenty of sand to assure solid coverage. (See illustration for examples of dune lines.)

Examples of Dune Lines

6" by 12" oaktag or cardboard

Paint area below dune lines with white glue and cover glued area with sand

Pick up your mini-dune collage carefully and tap the back to remove any loose grains of sand. Allow it to dry for about fifteen minutes in the sun.

To make your seascape really come to life, we'll add some "salty" details.

Adding the Details

Select from your collection of beach debris a few of the most interesting items. Perhaps a scallop shell, a twig of driftwood, a gull feather, and some dried grass tufts. Experiment for the best combination of items. Arrange them attractively and glue each one onto the collage. Don't worry about any white glue showing. It will dry clear. Do not clutter your collage with too many details. Keep the ideas simple.

You can tear a small circle of orange or yellow construction paper and paste it above your dunes to represent the sun (or moon, if you have sprayed an evening sky).

With your black marker, draw several gulls winging their way through the sky and, perhaps, write a short phrase or poem that sums up your emotions about a wild ocean beach.

(See illustration.) There! The beach is forever yours!

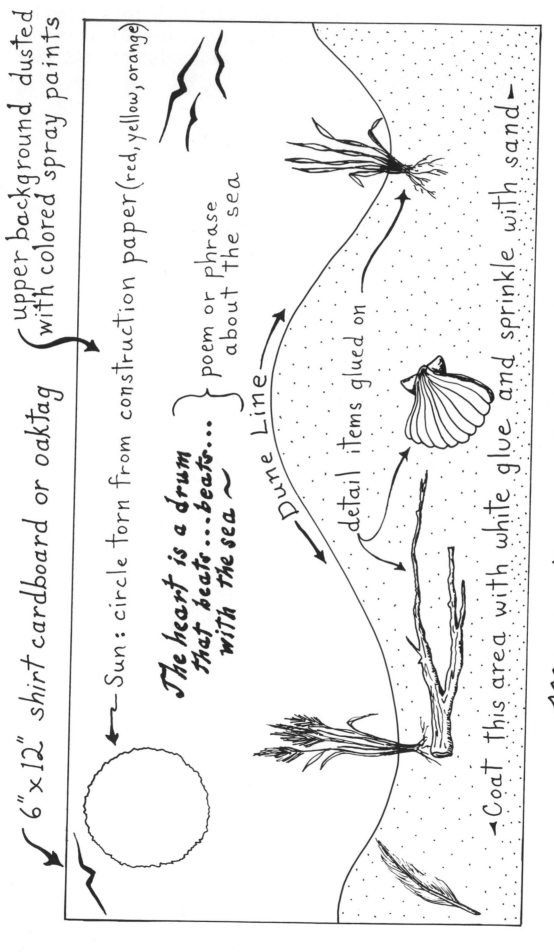

6" x 12" shirt cardboard or oaktag

upper background dusted with colored spray paints

Sun: circle torn from construction paper (red, yellow, orange)

The heart is a drum that beats ...beats... with the sea ~

poem or phrase about the sea

Dune Line

detail items glued on

Coat this area with white glue and sprinkle with sand

Mini ~ Dune Collage

STARFISH SANTA CLAUS

Are you a person who enjoys autumn walks along the seashore, natural crafts, and Christmas? Of course you are! And here's an idea that will allow you to combine all three activities to produce a unique and nature-oriented Christmas ornament...Starfish Santa Claus!

Of course, you'll need starfish. Fewer people visit the ocean beaches from October through November. Yet, this is the time when wave action increases. (December is great if you don't mind the chill.) These waves throw thousands of young starfish upon the beach. Most are perfect in shape and vary in size from two to four inches across.

Collect them by the dozens. You will please clammers and oystermen since starfish are primary predators of these delicious shellfish. Take the starfish home and lay them on a flat surface outdoors, in the sun, for about five days or until thoroughly dry and stiff. Turn the starfish over each day as they are drying and, if you have cats in your neighborhood, it is a good idea to cover them with a protective wire screen.

Next, follow the directions for painting as shown in the illustration. Use a small fine-tipped brush and inexpensive non-toxic poster paints. You will need only red, black, and white. Let each color dry before proceeding to the next.

Now, it's time to prepare your ornaments for hanging. Turn your starfish over, painted side down. Use a sharp needle and, from the *back*, gently poke a hole through the middle of the starfish arm that is Santa's cap. Push the needle into the natural hollow between the rows of tiny tentacles.

Finally, take a short length of thread (gold or silver is prettiest) and pass it through the hole. Tie the ends to form a small loop. Snip off the loose ends close to the knot.

11

These starfish also look beautiful when spray-painted in gold, silver, or copper colors and make fine additions to wreaths. Be creative....Have fun!

Well? What are you waiting for? Go show it off....*then* hang it on your tree. And Merry Christmas!

Starfish Santa Claus Ornament

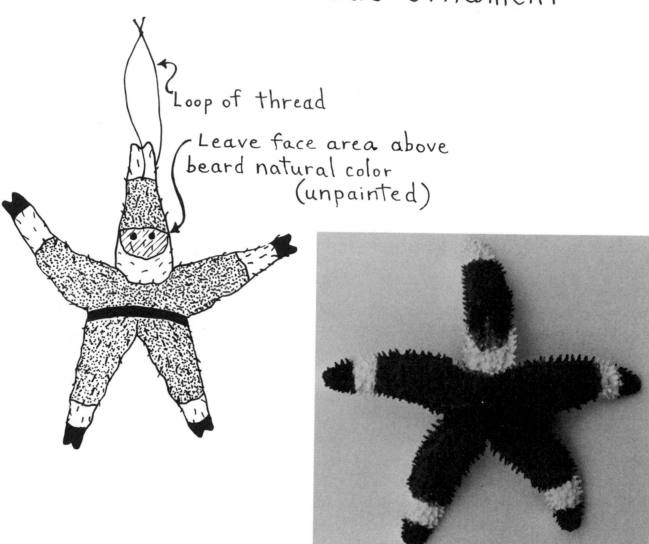

Loop of thread

Leave face area above beard natural color (unpainted)

■ Black: boots, gloves, belt, and eyes

☐ White: beard, top of cap, and all cuffs

▨ Red: suit and lower part of cap

GULL FEATHER PENS

No beach seems quite complete without its graceful gulls. The beauty of their silent glides and wind-bourne cries are a comforting bonus whenever we visit the sea.

Gulls can provide another enjoyable bonus — their feathers — if you know what to do with them. Here's one good idea.

Gulls, like all other birds, periodically lose their feathers, one or two at a time, to be replaced by new feathers. This process is called *molting*. As you walk the beach, pick up any large feathers you find. You will want feathers with a long thick shaft. You'll be making a quill pen similar to those used by our early American ancestors.

Rinse the feathers under cold water until clean. Gently blot them dry with a paper towel.

The key to a good quill pen is in properly cutting the tip. You will need a sharp hobby knife, such as an X-ACTO knife. These are inexpensive and come with interchangeable blades. Be careful in your use of this tool. It is razor sharp.

To form your writing point, you must make three separate cuts. Refer to the diagram to see the method and order for each of these cuts.

Gull Feather Pen

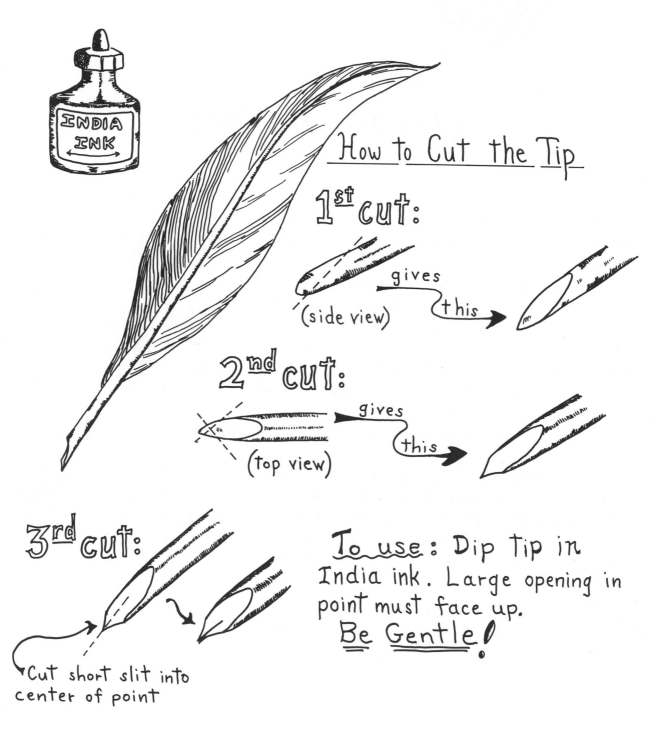

INDIA INK

How to Cut the Tip

1st cut:

(side view)

gives this →

2nd cut:

(top view)

gives this →

3rd cut:

Cut short slit into center of point

To use: Dip tip in India ink. Large opening in point must face up.
Be Gentle!

Using the Pen

With your point properly cut, dip the tip of the pen into India ink. (India ink is available in many colors and is permanent.) Dip the point up to the end of the large opening (1st cut) you made in the shaft.

To write, hold the quill with the large opening facing up. This area acts as an ink "reservoir." The ink will flow through the slit (3rd cut) you made in the point.

Be gentle. Be patient. These are delicate pens and it takes practice to use them properly. Hold the pen at a forty-five degree angle to the paper and use delicate pressure as you write.

Children of colonial times used quill pens (usually made from turkey feathers) and, like pencils, they occasionally had to be re-sharpened. Or, in the case of a quill pen, re-cut. When the feather shaft became too short to be re-cut, the pen was thrown away.

Your writing may require blotting to help it dry faster. Do you know what was often used for this task? SAND! That's right. Bring some back from the beach. In colonial times, a tin shaker was filled with fine sand. The freshly written letter was placed in a shallow tray and sand was sprinkled over the surface of the paper to absorb any heavy blobs of ink. The letter was removed and the loose sand was shaken off.

You can make your gull feather pen more colorful by dipping the entire feather in bright aniline dyes. Aniline dyes can be bought at any drugstore, fabric shop, or department store. Follow the simple package instructions.

Have fun with your pen...and write a thank-you note to the gulls!

STONE BEAST OR ROCKASAURUS

They're hiding everywhere around you....At the beach...in the woods...and by the roadsides. They wait quietly to be discovered. Your first glance will tell you they're only ordinary stones. But look closely! With a bit of imagination and some constructive fun, you can supply the magic needed to bring life to these common rocks. Yes, YOU can create a beast of stone!

Here's a stimulating and creative nature art that will allow your imagination to run wild as you produce that rare beast, the rockasaurus. If you're ready to play the role of a mad scientist, let's begin.

Step I - A Rock Hunt

Take a walk and collect a wide assortment of stones. Limit the size of the stones to fist-size and smaller. Select stones of any strange shape or color that might suggest the head, body, legs, tail, or other body parts of any animal. Pebbles, tiny stones, or even sticks may be used for eyes, ears, noses, tails, beaks, or other small appendages. A series of flat circular stones in decending size order makes a great snake when glued together. The animals you choose to create, of course, can be highly whimsical in design.

Take time to experiment with many stones to find a set that fits well together as a unit. Try different possibilities of heads, bodies, and legs. Rotate or reverse stones for the most interesting appearance and best fit. When you have decided on your set of stones, label each part lightly in pencil. For example: RFL for right front leg, H for head, and T for tail. It's important for a scientist to be organized, even "mad" ones! Besides, you may easily confuse unlabeled stones that look similar.

Keep the parts of your "monster-to-be" safely together in a plastic bag.

Step II - Construction Materials

Every good scientist has a well-equipped lab. Here's what you will need, professor, to assemble your monster.

- Plasticene (non-hardening) modeling clay
- Elmer's white glue
- Tempera paints (assorted colors) and a small brush
- Magic marker pens (assorted colors)
- Cloth tape or masking tape

Step III - Assembly and Painting

You are now ready to bring your creature to life. This operation will require patience and care.

Apply white glue liberally to the faces of stone parts, such as the head and body, where they will be in contact with each other. White glue provides a surprisingly strong bond and dries clear. Keep the stones from moving as they set by pressing a band of clay around them. The clay will *not* be held by the glue and can be easily removed when the glue has dried. You may also use highly adhesive cloth tape or masking tape but they will bond with the glue and may be difficult to remove. If you decide to use tape, be sure no glue drips or runs from the rock joinings onto the tape.

Do not rush the gluing of the stones. Let the head set thoroughly before going on to glue other parts. (White glue takes a couple of hours to set firmly and dries completely in a day.)

When assembly is complete, you have the choice of leaving your stone monster or rockasaurus in its natural state or painting it. Tempera paints and fine brushes are quite effective. Spray paints work well. Magic markers are excellent for adding details such as spots, stripes, eyelashes, or eyes. (See photos for examples.)

"Slag" by Charles Lellig, age 12   **Rock Pig by Nicole Michalski, age 12**

Stone Beasts

Mouse and Cheese by Denise Sinnott, age 11

Duck by the author

Rabbit by Antonia Noto, age 12

To make neat, even, fine-edged lines or stripes on your creation, try using thinly cut strips of tape. Press them onto your animal's body in the desired pattern. Paint over them and carefully lift the strips. The areas between the tape will appear as solid stripes.

Find a spot where your beast can stand proudly, for all the world (at least your family) to see. As an extension to your work, why not write an exciting tale about your beast and the dangers you braved in creating it?

For other ideas....Create an entire menagerie...Use them as paperweights or gifts to friends...or build a scenic diorama for your creation.

Congratulations on your successful operation, Professor!

WHELK (CONCH) PLANTER

Many of us collect shells. We marvel at their vast array of delicate colors, textures, and flowing curves.

A beautiful shell, placed in a sunlit window, can grace any room. But here's how to have your shells perform a function and be aesthetically pleasing at the same time. You're going to make a hanging shell planter.

A favorite find of beachwalkers is a large perfect shell of a whelk or conch. And they *can* be quite large. Eight inches is common but one southern species, the Florida horse conch, can grow to two feet in length!

These animals are abundant and their shells are readily found, washed ashore. Most conches eat algae. Whelks are carnivorous (meat-eating) animals and feed on clams, oysters, or other shellfish by drilling through their shells with a raspy tongue-like structure. So, catch a whelk, save a clam!

If you have trouble finding an empty whelk shell in good condition on the beach, try a local fish market. Whelks and conches are prepared and sold as seafood. They are a popular food with Europeans and are often marketed under the name "scungilli." Or, if you live near a harbor, ask a lobsterman for a few shells, as whelk commonly enter their baited lobster pots.

Once you have your shell, wash it well. This is the only preparation necessary unless you wish a high luster on your planter. In that case, brush or spray a coat of clear varnish over the outside of the shell and allow it to dry overnight.

The inside of your shell will be filled with loose potting soil or sand to 1/2 inch below the lip of the opening.

The choice of plants, of course, is entirely up to you but to keep your planter really "beachy," try selecting a plant representative of the shore. A good example is dusty miller, a pale-green wooly-leaved dune plant that raises a shaft of yellow flowers from July to September. It is now sold for rock gardens or as a border plant at many garden shops and nurseries. (It is not a good idea to deplete the dunes of these plants, as they promote dune growth, and the dunes act as protective barriers against ocean storm waves.)

Another good choice is beach pea with its purple flowers and edible seed pods.

To hang your whelk shell planter you'll need a one inch brass curtain ring and two twenty-four inch lengths of colored yarn.

Knot the four ends of the yarn to the ring so that two equal loops hang from the ring. (See illustration.) Do not pull the knots tight until you have slipped your shell into the loops and checked to see if it hangs properly. You may have to make small adjustments to have your shell hang level. (See illustration.)

Whelk shells have natural curves, knobs, and ridges that will prevent the yarn from slipping off but you may wish to secure the yarn to the underside of the shell with a drop of white glue.

Slide the ring over a hook or nail for a unique display.

That's it! And no more hanging around....That's a job for your whelk shell planter!

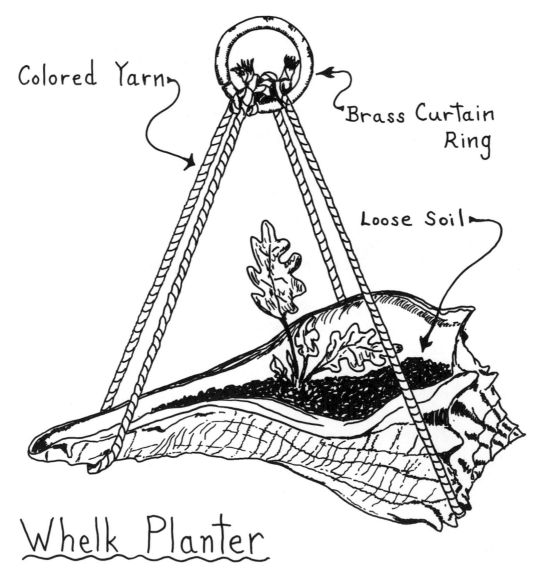

Colored Yarn

Brass Curtain Ring

Loose Soil

Whelk Planter

SEAWEED MOUNTINGS

You sit by a small tidal pool. The sea washes in and out rhythmically. Beneath the water's surface, your eyes are caught by feathery tufts, delicate blue-green ribbons, and slender red filaments undulating to the beat of the ocean. The dancelike motions of these plants are hypnotic and you are soon peacefully adrift within yourself....Your mind floats free....Troubled thoughts disappear.

The plants creating this experience are lumped into the catch-all category of "seaweed." A weed is defined as an unwanted plant. In fact, "seaweed" refers to the thousands of forms of marine algae, and they are both beautiful and important, providing oxygen, food, and shelter to small marine organisms.

You can capture the beauty of these marine plants in a simple art form as delicate as a Chinese silk painting.

You will need a shallow rectangular pan about two to three inches deep (a cake pan works well), a packet of 5" by 8" unlined index cards, a small knife, and tweezers.

Most marine algae are gelatinous plants. Because of this naturally sticky gel within the plant, no glue will be needed to mount your specimens.

Marine algae, or seaweed, come in many shades of green, blue-green, red, and brown. (They are grouped scientifically by these colors.) Once mounted, your seaweed will retain its natural color.

You can complete your seaweed mountings on the beach but you may wish to work in the comfort of your home. If so, take a covered container to the beach and half-fill it with sea water.

Using your knife, gently scrape or slice a variety of algae from the rocks or pier pilings and drop them into your container. Many fine samples, like sea lettuce or mermaid's hair, can be found floating free in the water, torn loose by the surf.

Bring your collected samples home and prepare a work area. Pour about two inches of sea water into the shallow pan. With the tweezers, select a single seaweed sample and float it in the pan.

Take a 5" by 8" index card and slip it into the water beneath the seaweed. The seaweed sample may have to be trimmed if too large for the card.

Use the tweezers to separate, spread, and arrange the filaments of the seaweed. Slowly, raise the index card and allow the plant to settle onto the paper. Excess water will run off. (Refer to the illustration.)

Seaweed Mounting

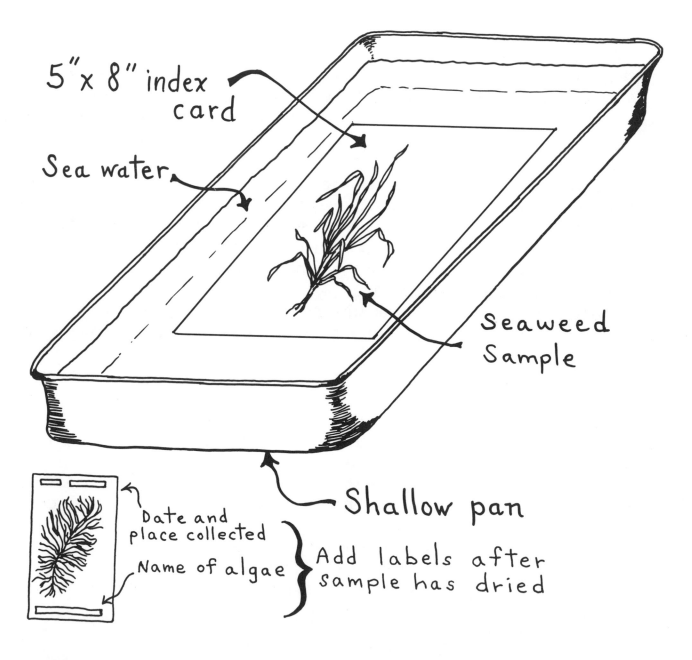

5" x 8" index card

Sea water

Seaweed Sample

Shallow pan

Date and place collected

Name of algae

} Add labels after sample has dried

You can make final adjustments to the seaweed at this time, if need be.

Place the card on a flat absorbent surface to dry. Try a desk blotter or a layer of newspaper on a counter or tabletop. If you are working on the beach, place them on the sand in the sun.

When your mountings are dry, they can be labeled and even framed. (See photos for examples of finished cards.) Your local library or bookshop can provide you with a field guide to seashore life. It will be an easy job to identify your algae.

Seaweed Mountings

Kelp
(Laminaria)
Brown Algae

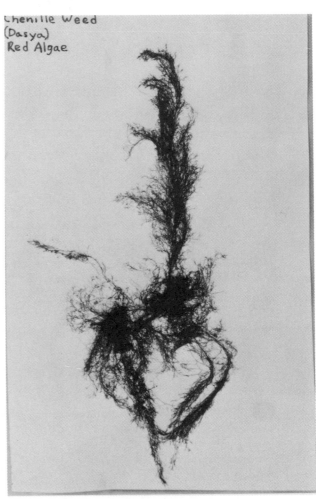

Chenille Weed
(Dasya)
Red Algae

Heavier forms of seaweed with thick branching stalks do not mount well. They must be dried first and later glued (white glue).

For an interesting twist, try mounting two or three different algae on the same card in an attractive arrangement.

Well, that's it....And I "sea weed" better move on to our next activity!

SUN PRINTS

Did you ever take pictures without a camera?

"Impossible!" you say?

Not so. With some simple materials and a good eye for artistic composition, this activity will involve you in a photographic process that can produce spectacular results.

Here's a list of what you'll need:

- 10" by 13" piece of cardboard
- 9" by 12" pane of glass
- masking tape
- black heavy duty plastic trash bag
- shallow baking pan or tray about 2 or 3 inches deep
- some coarse gravel
- a package of blueprint paper (ask for DIAZO paper, 245-medium speed)

The blueprint paper is available at blueprint, drafting, and architectural supply shops. It is quite inexpensive and can be purchased in packages of 250 sheets. Do not open the package until you are ready to use it. The paper is extremely sun-sensitive and can be affected by humidity, for which reason it is sold in sealed plastic wrappers.

Building the "Camera"

With a heavy marking pen and ruler, draw a rectangular outline of 8 inches by 10 inches on the cardboard sheet. The items you choose to "photograph" or sunprint should be carefully composed within these guidelines.

Tape the edges of the glass pane with two layers of masking tape for safety. Your "camera" is now complete. Check the diagram to confirm your results.

Assembling the "Darkroom"

In the shallow tray or baking pan, place a level inch of coarse gravel. Aquarium gravel works well, as does chipped bluestone often used in driveways.

Pour some *clear* household ammonia into the gravel but be sure *not* to let the liquid rise above the gravel. (A half inch of ammonia is sufficient.)

Slip the tray inside the heavy duty black plastic trash bag and close it tightly. Do not flatten the bag. Allow enough air space within the bag so that it balloons out slightly. You can hold the bag closed with spring clothespins or rubber bands. If you are working with a friend, one of you may hold the bag closed by hand while the other is exposing a sunprint. Either way, you do not want the ammonia fumes to escape as they are the chemical means by which your sunprints will be photographically fixed. Compare your darkroom with the diagram.

Sunprints

Sunprinting Set~up

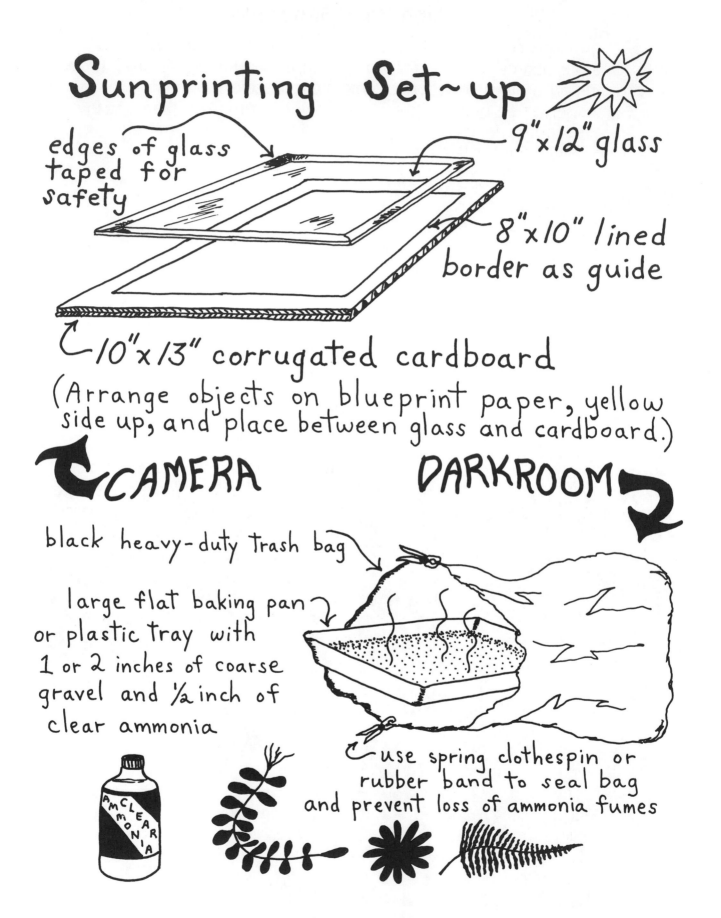

edges of glass taped for safety

9"x12" glass

8"x10" lined border as guide

10"x13" corrugated cardboard

(Arrange objects on blueprint paper, yellow side up, and place between glass and cardboard.)

CAMERA   DARKROOM

black heavy-duty trash bag

large flat baking pan or plastic tray with 1 or 2 inches of coarse gravel and ½ inch of clear ammonia

CLEAR AMMONIA

use spring clothespin or rubber band to seal bag and prevent loss of ammonia fumes

Making Your Sunprint

Sunprinting is really a method of profiling objects in contrasts of blue and white. Opaque objects that lie flat on the paper work best, as they produce sharp definition around their edges and deeper color contrasts. Try leaves, shells, coins, grasses, pine needles, and flowers. Ferns and plants with compound leaves such as locust or winged sumac produce dramatic results. Thicker items will print with fuzzy edges for an attractive soft focus look.

Do not open your sunprint paper yet. Your first step is to collect and arrange the objects you wish to print.

Using the cardboard sheet and glass pane, assemble and compose your materials within the rectangular border. The glass serves two purposes. It will prevent the wind from blowing away or otherwise disturbing your arrangement of delicate leaves or flowers. It also helps to flatten the items for sharper photographic definition.

In the deep shade, (perhaps under a nearby tree,) carefully open the package of DIAZO blueprint paper at one end. Set the cardboard on the ground. Remove your items and place them in the same arrangement on the ground next to the cardboard. Quickly slip out a single sheet of blueprint paper. Place it on the cardboard over the guidelines with the *yellow or tinted side up.* Try to work quickly. Re-assemble your materials on top of the blueprint paper and place the glass pane over them.

Carry the whole assembly into the bright sunlight and set it down carefully. In 7 to 15 seconds, depending upon the intensity of the sunlight, the print paper will turn from pale yellow to pure white. The paper is now fully exposed. Pick up your camera and return to your plastic bag darkroom in the shade.

Slide your sunprint out from under the glass and materials and slip it quickly into the plastic bag. Close the bag tightly. Allow the print to remain in the bag for a full minute, or two, to give the ammonia fumes a chance to fully work on your sunprint. Then, remove it and be amazed! These prints are worthy of framing.

This activity can be done by groups as well as individuals. You will need to assemble additional cameras, but the plastic bag darkroom can accommodate and develop many prints at once.

If you are developing many prints, occasionally add fresh ammonia to the gravel pan to keep the fumes at full strength. Otherwise, the results achieved in the developing process will be poor.

Remember, ammonia fumes are an irritant to eyes and nasal membranes. Keep the bag and bottle closed tightly during this activity.

Your blueprint paper cannot be stored indefinitely. The chemical components of the paper will slowly break down within a year. If you do store your paper for shorter periods, be sure it is sealed tightly again in its black plastic wrapper and placed in a dry, cool, dark closet or cabinet.

Now, there's a blueprint for artistic success!

3-D BEACH AND DUNE MURAL

This activity, aside from producing a large-scale collage, will enable anyone to learn about the physical construction, life forms, and dynamics of an ocean beach. It makes for an exciting, attractive, and valuable class science project where students can develop and sharpen skills in observation, identification, classification, and collection. Finally, they will design and reconstruct a model beach.

The complete beach is made up of several zones. These zones include the ocean's edge, the lower beach, the upper beach, (beyond the high tide line,) and then the primary dune, the swale, the secondary dune and finally the uplands. The swale is an area of low elevation, a protected hollow, between the dunes. By reducing the geography of the beach to a six-foot cross-section on mural paper, we readily see the relationships and contrasts within the various zones that make up the ocean beach.

The mural paper, also called "craft" paper, is sold on rolls three feet wide. It is sold at art supply shops in a wide range of colors. You will want to use either white or manila. Buy a piece at least six feet long. I like my murals of impressive size. I use two sheets, each three feet by eight feet, with the lower edge of one sheet taped to the upper edge of the other sheet. My working surface is now six feet by eight feet and provides ample space for mounting many specimens and labels.

Another source for your craft paper is the local school art room. No elementary art instructor worth their sea salt would be without it.

Outlining the Mural

There are two common geological constructions of ocean beaches. Illustrations follow. Study them and choose the one that is most typical of your area. In a barrier beach, the mainland proper is protected from the pounding ocean surf by a narrow offshore spit of sand or island. A sheltered bay or lagoon lies between the island and the coast of the mainland. Some areas may include a salt marsh.

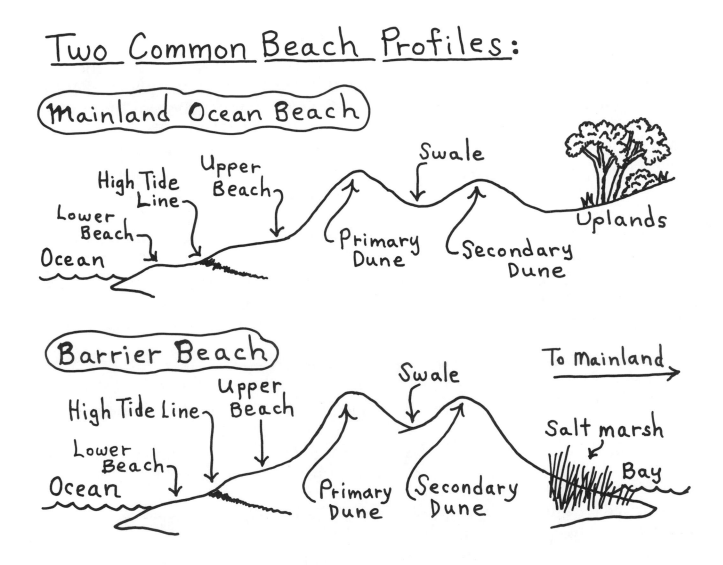

Two Common Beach Profiles:

Mainland Ocean Beach

Ocean · Lower Beach · High Tide Line · Upper Beach · Primary Dune · Swale · Secondary Dune · Uplands

Barrier Beach

Ocean · Lower Beach · High Tide Line · Upper Beach · Primary Dune · Swale · Secondary Dune · To mainland · Salt marsh · Bay

On your craft paper, draw a light pencil outline of the appropriate beach profile for your area. When you are satisfied with the shape of your sketch, trace over the lines with a wide black felt-tip marking pen.

Using tempera paints and water, prepare thin color washes of pale yellow, light blue, and dark blue. Spread washes over the mural with a soft 1" brush. Use yellow for the dunes, light blue for the sky, and dark blue for the sea.

Print neat labels for each beach zone on white unlined index cards and glue them in their proper places on the mural. You may paint a sun in the sky or cut one out of yellow construction paper. Your mural needs clouds. Tear odd shapes from cotton rolls or use portions of aquarium filter floss. Glue them onto the sky and fluff them out to create depth in your mural.

The mural is now ready to receive mounted specimens but first you'll have to collect them.

Specimen Collecting

Each zone of the beach is unique unto itself. Specialized plants and animals exist in these narrow ecosystems. Bring with you to the shore at least six collecting bags. I prefer heavy paper sacks of the type used in packing your groceries at the supermarket. Line each one with a kitchen size plastic trash bag. This prevents damp specimens from weakening the paper bags.

Label each bag clearly with a marking pen for a specific beach zone. Bring a small plant clipper and a sheath knife as aids in obtaining specimens. Many beach grasses have razor edges and can cause nasty cuts if they are pulled by hand. So, use the clippers. The knife can pry loose barnacles or dried algae from large stones.

There are some important points to remember in collecting plant and animal specimens at the shore. Follow these basic guidelines:

    (1) Never uproot beach plants. They are important to the dune bulding process.

    (2) Take only one clipping from each different plant.

    (3) Some dune areas are protected by law. Check first.

    (4) Do not collect animal remains like crab shells if they still contain soft fleshy material. Your nose will thank you.

    (5) Do not collect live sea animals unless you have a salt water aquarium set up and a way to transport the animals home safely from the beach.

    (6) Collect only what you will really use. Keep your sampling light. You have to carry it.

Begin your walk at the lower beach. Let your eyes sweep the ground before you. Become a real beachcomber. Pick up a little of everything, (sand, driftwood, beach glass, algae, coal, shells, crab moltings, sponges, bones, feathers, plants, and even litter.) You will identify them prior to mounting. Some excellent source books for this task are suggested in the next step.

Completing the Mural

Spread your mural flat out on the floor. (On a nice day, you may wish to work outdoors on the lawn or on your driveway.) Empty the collected specimens out, one bag at a time, over their appropriate areas on the mural. Select and arrange the best items in an eye-pleasing display. Work through each zone and, when you are satisfied with the layout, glue each object down with a moderate blob of white glue. Do this to affix your plant specimens, too. While the glue is drying, you can begin the identification and label-making process.

If you are a budding naturalist, well-experienced in botany or marine science, you can create and paste down your labels immediately. For most, however, the learning experience will continue through the use of reference or source books on the seashore. The following suggested books contain clear text, straightforward descriptions, and accurate illustrations to make the task of identification a simple one. They will prove to be a valuable addition to any personal library. Of course, you can borrow these texts from your school or public library. A more extensive bibliography appears at the end of this book.

— Suggested Seashore Guide Books —

Amos, William H. *Life of the Seashore.*
New York: McGraw Hill, 1966.

Crowder, William. *Seashore Life Between the Tides.*
New York: Dover Publications, 1975.

Gosner, Kenneth L. *A Field Guide to the Atlantic Seashore.*
Boston: Houghton Mifflin Co., 1979.

Miner, R.W. *Field Book of Seashore Life.*
New York: G.P. Putnam's Sons, 1950.

Petry, Loren C. and Marcia G. Norman. *A Beachcomber's Botany.*
Chatham: The Chatham Conservation Foundation, Inc., 1968.

Sterling, Dorothy. *The Outer Lands.*
New York: W.W. Norton & Co., Inc., 1978.

You might also try the handy Golden Field Guide series on shells, the seashore, and fishes.

After all your identification labels are completed, brush any bare beach or dune areas on the mural with thinned white glue, (1 part glue to 1 part water,) and sprinkle them liberally with dry sand. Allow the mural to dry for an hour or two.

Finally, carry the mural outdoors and hold it vertically. Tap the mural to remove loose sand particles and it's ready for display. (Use plenty of tape or staples!)

The illustration suggests one possibility for a finished 3-D Beach and Dune Mural.

3-D Beach and Dune Mural

(Illustration shows cross-section of a barrier beach.)
Glue labels, plant samples, shells, etc., onto the area where they were found with white glue.

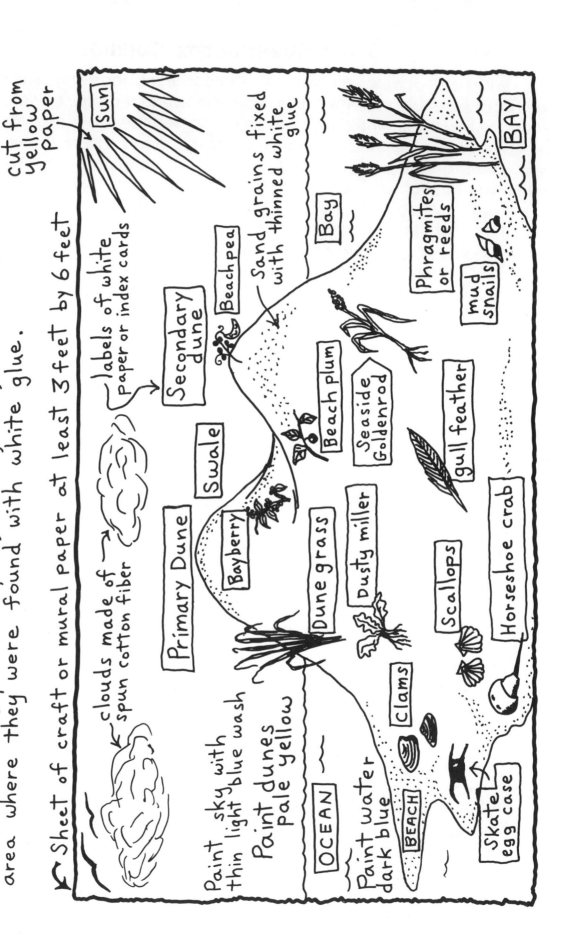

← Sheet of craft or mural paper at least 3 feet by 6 feet

labels of white paper or index cards

clouds made of spun cotton fiber

Paint sky with thin light blue wash

Paint dunes pale yellow

OCEAN

Paint water dark blue

BEACH

Skate egg case

Clams

Dusty miller

Dune grass

Scallops

Horseshoe crab

Seaside Goldenrod

gull feather

Beach plum

Bayberry

Primary Dune

Swale

Secondary dune

Beach pea

Sun

cut from yellow paper

Sand grains fixed with thinned white glue

Bay

BAY

Phragmites or reeds

mud snails

Some Questions to Consider

With your mural complete, it should be obvious that each plant form prefers a particular zone in which it can thrive and reproduce. Perhaps you also found evidence of land mammals in the form of deer or rabbit droppings.

The ocean beach is a beautiful, but harsh, environment. Plants and animals are exposed to chilling winter storms, high winds, summer heat, intense sunlight, and air borne salt spray.

What unique qualities does each plant possess that enable it to adapt and survive here? How do they manage to retain water? Are the leaves or stems of the plant special in any way? Why do certain plants exist in the swale zone and not on the dunes?

What about the animals? Which zone gave the greatest evidence of mammal life? How do these mammals obtain fresh water? Do you think any of the plants are a food source for animals? If so, which ones?

Finally, if your life depended upon it, do you believe you could exist in an ocean beach or barrier beach environment?

Shape and Texture Scavenger Hunt

Did you ever notice how folks at the beach just love to push and wiggle their toes and fingers through the sand? Why do we do it? Because it feels good! The soft warmth comforts us and, maybe, reminds us of that little wooden sandbox in which we used to play.

The beach is just chock full of interesting shapes to see and surfaces to touch, all provided by nature.

The activity sheet on the following page will be your excuse to discover these textures and shapes, while providing a chance to practice your adjectives.

As you walk along the beach, collect natural objects that can be described by one of the adjectives in the boxes. You should be able to find an item for each word. Use a sharp eye and your imagination. Perhaps you can find an object that is described by three words at once.

Mount your collected items on cardboard or plywood. Cut out or copy the words as labels and paste them beneath your collection of textures and shapes. And don't be touchy about showing your work!

Shape and Texture Scavenger Hunt

FUZZY	HARD
SCRATCHY	CURLY
POINTY	FLAT
SOFT	Smooth
THIN	HOLLOW
BUMPY	HAIRY
POROUS	FLEXIBLE

Collect items to represent each texture or shape.
Mount objects on plywood or cardboard with white glue.
Cut out labels and paste beneath each object.

BEACH BINGO

This outdoor form of bingo will boost your powers of observation and knowledge in finding and identifying objects on the beach. The grid on the next page contains twenty-five squares, each naming a specific item to be found. Remember that the beach is divided into zones, and the items listed may be found from the sea's edge to beyond the dunes. Bring along a general seashore field guide and use the book's index to locate illustrated pages for items with which you may not be familiar. Good luck.

Variation: Scavenger Board Bingo

On a piece of plywood or cardboard about two feet square, draw a neat grid of twenty-five squares, five boxes across and five boxes down. Write the names of items to be found in the upper part of each box. Find the objects names and affix a sample in each box with tape or glue. You will have to substitute for some items named on the original beach bingo sheet. After all, you can't be expected to pluck poison ivy...and gluing a gull onto your sheet could cause it to become "fly" paper.

BEACH BINGO

When you see objects named on this sheet, place an "x" in that square. One winner each for a diagonal, vertical, or horizontal row. Complete all squares to be grand champion!

Blue Mussel	Beach Plum	Moon Snail Shell	Seaside Goldenrod	Oyster Shell
Slipper Shell	Red Beach Pebble	Common Tern	Crab Claw	Beach Pea Plant
Horse Shoe Crab	Feather	Litter	Salt Spray Rosebush	Gull
Clam Shell	Poison Ivy	Scallop	Dusty miller Plant	Animal Bone
Drift Wood	Evidence of a Fire	Dune Grass	Algae	Bayberry Bush

Use your field guides...

CLAMSHELL CANDY OR JEWELRY DISH

We all have a catch-all receptacle somewhere in the house. Perhaps it's a souvenir ashtray or a small glass bowl on the dresser top into which we toss our spare change, cufflinks, or earrings. Or maybe you have a dainty candy dish on the coffee table for guests. If so, try this creative idea for recycling empty clam shells to produce a most unique and attractive candy dish.

From a set of clamshells, select two that complement each other well regarding shape, size, and color.

Wash the shells well. Scrub them, inside and out, with a soapy steel wool scouring pad. Rinse them thoroughly.

Polish them with a pasty mixture of any non-bleaching scouring powder and a soft rag. Rinse them well and towel off any excess water. Allow them to dry completely for an hour in the sun.

If your shells have any chipped edges or sharp nicks, smooth them down with a fine-toothed file or some medium grade sandpaper. Blow off or wipe away any dust particles on the shells.

To assemble the dish, you will glue the shells back to back. The shell with the most colorful interior should be on top as the dish. The other shell is your base.

Place the base shell down on a flat surface. On the highest point on the back of this shell, apply a small blob of household cement or epoxy. Do the same on the back of the upper dish where it will be in contact with the base. Assemble the shells. Hold them in proper alignment for a few minutes until the glue begins to set. Or, you may hold the shells in position with a piece of masking tape. Remove this when the glue has dried.

Take a length of twisted jute or hemp rope, the type used in macramé work, and wrap it around the joining of the shells. Cut the rope to exact size and glue it in place as shown in the illustration. Your work will take on a real nautical flair if your braid the rope first or tie it around the join with a simple seafaring knot. Try a square knot.

Clamshell Jewelry or Candy Dish

Shells joined with white glue or epoxy

Wash and polish two large surf clam shells. After glue has set, spray with clear varnish or lacquer.

twisted jute or hemp cord, tied or glued around joining of clam shells, back~to~back

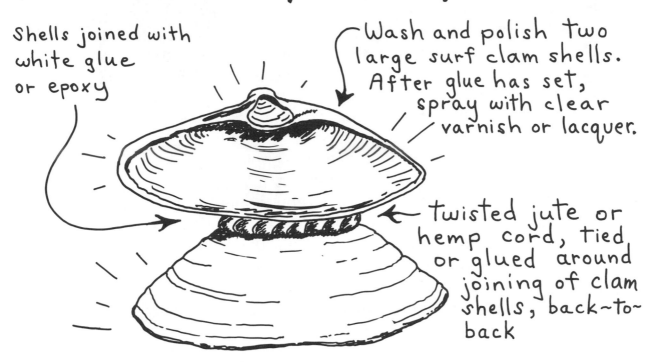

As a finishing touch, we want to give our dish a brilliant shine. Use a high quality varnish and apply several coats. The varnish will not only produce a glossy finish, it will deepen the colors and accent the lines within the shell just as it does with the grain in wood.

I prefer to brush the varnish on with a soft half-inch brush. I find it easier to reach the nooks and crannies of the shells and rope with a brush. However, spray cans of varnish are available and they work well. Whichever method you choose, do not try to cut corners and save time by spreading one heavy coat of varnish on your work. Three or four light coats produce dazzling results. The first coat seals the shell's porous surface. The following coats bring on the deep shine. Let each coat dry fully between applications. With some products this may mean up to eight hours. Be patient. It's worth it.

Once you've mastered this craft, you might find that people will be more than willing to pay for your work at gift shops or local craft fairs.

You might also consider decorating your upper shell with a mock scrimshaw design before the varnishing. (See the activity, "Clamshell Scrimshaw," describing this technique.)

Nicely done! Your work is a shining example of seashore art.

BEACH PEBBLE MOSAIC

The stones and pebbles strewn about the seashore contain a magnificent variety of colors and designs. There are rich hues of red and yellow, brilliant whites and soft grays. You will find purple, black, and brown. The stones may be striped, speckled, or mottled, and they have been tumbled and polished by the waves and sand. These seashore jewels will provide the raw materials for a beach pebble mosaic, a picture patterned in glued stones.

Collecting pebbles takes no special skill, but they must be sorted into colored sets as they are gathered. Take a basket or pail and set six to eight, cut-down, quart milk containers inside. Use one container for each color of pebble you choose to collect. Collect as many as is reasonable, but you will need a fair number.

Take pebbles of various sizes and shapes. Collect some very small ones but do not use pebbles larger than your thumbnail.

On a piece of oaktag or cardboard, outline your mosaic pattern lightly in pencil. Keep your theme simple and uncluttered. Try a starfish, a whale, or even a sailboat, as shown in the illustrated example.

Be inventive and daring with your color scheme. Remember that water does not have to be blue and a sun needs not be yellow.

Position the pebbles onto the pattern for a good fit. Then, use drops of white glue to cement the pebbles onto the sheet in tightly-fitted clusters. Work with one color at a time. Complete the details of the main subject first. Work from the inside of the picture to the edges. Complete the background last.

Let the glue dry thoroughly and spray your mosaic with two light coats of varnish or shellac. You can display your finished work in a matte board frame.

Beach pebble mosaics also look beautiful on driftwood or on stained pine boards. Try colored oaktag sheets, too.

If, at any time, you're unable to get to the beach and the urge to do a mosaic strikes,...don't panic. Visit any local pet shop that deals in aquarium supplies. They stock gravel and pebbles in several sizes and in a wide range of deep colors.

Let's get cracking.

Beach Pebble Mosaic

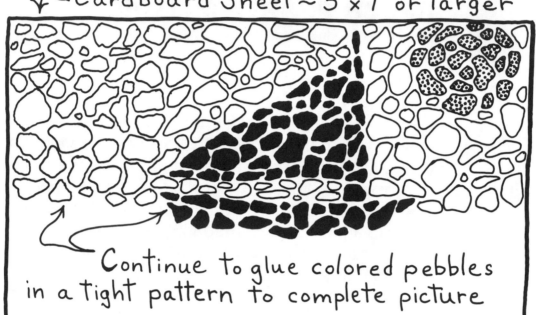

~Cardboard Sheet ~ 5"x 7" or larger

Continue to glue colored pebbles in a tight pattern to complete picture

Sample color code: ☐ yellow ■ black ▦ red

Outline your idea lightly in pencil. Complete one color at a time. Do the details first and the background last.

When the glue has dried, spray your mosaic with varnish or shellac.

Be creative!

THE ART OF SEINING

Perhaps the most exciting activity at the beach is that of capturing and observing live marine animals. You can occasionally pick up snails, pry loose a barnacle, or scoop a crab into a dipnet. And you can dig for clams. But what about those elusive shrimp and and fishes that thrive just off the shore? They are quick. They hide in the eelgrass and algae. Some even burrow into the sand. No problem. They can all be trapped in a seine net.

Seine nets, in various forms, are employed by commercial fishing vessels. Hand seining is accomplished with a long rectangular net stretched between two poles. It is walked through shallow water by two people.

In order to spread the net effectively in the water, the netting material is strung with weights along the bottom and floats along the top.

If you wish to make your own net, study the illustration for suggestions and directions. However, seine nets can be inexpensively purchased at sporting goods shops and fishing supply houses. They are complete, well-made, and will last for years with proper use. Check your telephone directory and look under "Nets" in the yellow pages.

Seine nets are sold in lengths from ten feet to thirty feet, with in-between sizes in multiples of five feet. A ten-foot seine does an excellent job and is easily handled by two children.

How to Construct a Seine Net

materials:

← 10 feet →

two broomsticks   heavy cord   a dozen fishing sinkers   netting or mesh material

cork floats or styrofoam balls

(top)

1. File grooves or drill holes at top and bottom of each broomstick. Distance between grooves must equal width of net. Cut the lower groove close to end of stick.

2. Secure four corners of net to poles with cord tied to grooves or holes.

3. At equal intervals of about 10 inches, tie sinkers along bottom edge of net with short lengths of cord. Punch holes in styrofoam balls with an awl or a pencil. Tie balls along top of net.

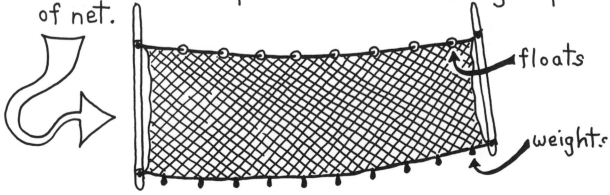

floats

weights

Using the Seine Net

There are a few simple, but important points to remember as you use the hand seine net. They are:

- Two people are needed to handle the poles. A third person may walk towards the outstretched net to drive fish into it.

- Walk *slowly* with the net. Let it form a broad arc in the water.

- Always walk *against* the current.

- Keep the bottoms of the poles tilted forward, away from you, and in contact with the sea bed. The net will more effectively sweep the bottom for ground-dwelling marine organisms.

- Have a large bucket or pan full of sea water ready on shore to receive your live specimens.

- For safety, *never* seine in the heavy ocean surf or in water deeper than your waist. Aside from the obvious danger, the net will not be productive. Seine in a sheltered bay or harbor.

The most abundant and varied catches are made in the waters near a salt marsh. This is the nursery of the sea where great numbers of fish spawn. It is where the complex marine food chain begins.

To seine, the pole handlers walk parallel to the shore for a short distance as shown in the illustration. The person closest to the shore line will then stop and pivot slowly as the partner walks in a wide sweep towards the shore. When the net is parallel to the shore, tilt the pole tops sharply back and walk the net onto the beach, stretched flat out like a bedsheet.

If you've made a good sweep, the net will be jumping with anything from eels to pipefish, shrimp to toadfish, and killies to crabs.

Quickly, but gently, pick the animals from the net and drop them into your collecting pan of sea water, where you can study and enjoy their behavior.

Do not worry about seining in an area where you can see no fish in the water. The reflected light on the water's surface obscures your vision and, thanks to nature's design, protective coloration makes most species all but invisible.

Using a Seine Net

- Walk <u>slowly</u> against the current
- Keep lower end of poles angled forward and in contact with the bay, creek, or stream bottom

Walk 20~30 yds.

slow wide sweep until net is parallel with shore

Direction of water current

Pivot

Shore Line

* For safety's sake, do not seine in deep water or heavy surf

Keep a pail or pan of water ready to receive your live specimens

floats

Lead weights

The assortment of marine creatures that find their way into your net will amaze you. And it will vary, month by month, with the migratory movements of the species. My own elementary students have caught hake, oyster toadfish, and mossbunker. For those hardy souls in wet suits, winter seining may net you some tasty tomcod.

Unfamiliar species will often be caught. Be sure you have a seashore field guide handy with a detailed section on fishes. An excellent one is *A Guide to Fishes of the Temperate Atlantic Coast* by Michael J. Ursin. Check the bibliography for other titles. Many are available on the market.

While observing your animals, add a fresh supply of sea water to your pan about every fifteen minutes. This will replenish the oxygen in the water and assure the health of your specimens. When you are done observing and identifying your animals, always return them safely to the sea.

If you plan to bring live specimens home for a saltwater aquarium, you'll need large containers with tight-fitting lids.

Many schools and delicatessens receive salads in five-gallon plastic pails with snap-on lids. Go to them. State your case and humbly ask for a couple. Scrub them out well but *do not use soap*. I've never found better containers for safely transporting my marine animals.

Fill the pails with sea water to within a few inches of the top. Include soil from the bay bottom and plenty of algae. Do not overcrowd the container with animals. Take only a few of each specimen. Fish, especially salt water varieties, require space.

After each sweep of the net, lift it, stretch it, and shake it out over the water. When you are done seining, swish the net clean in the water to remove any remaining bits of algae or small organisms. Then, roll it up neatly. It can be hosed down with fresh water at home, if necessary.

Your seine net can also be used in ponds, lakes, rivers, or streams. Follow the same procedures.

For related ideas, read the sections on "Saltwater Aquariums" and "Plankton Nets, Dip Nets, and Scoops."

PLANKTON NETS, DIP NETS, AND SCOOPS

The seine net is a fine tool for collecting marine specimens. But all tools have specific applications and limits to their use. As using the seine requires two people, it is of little value when you are alone. It can't be used from a pier, or in rocky tidal pools, or in narrow, backwater areas choked with marsh grasses. In addition, the open weave of the seine allows smaller, swimming organisms and plankton to escape and it is not effective in digging out burrowing forms of sea life such as the lugworm and sand lance.

Many of these small animals are unique in appearance and behavior, and will provide hours of rewarding observation. I have seen children (including myself) hypnotically fascinated by the acrobatic swimming of isopods.

Using the illustrations and directions that follow, you will construct a plankton net, a dip net, and a scoop; three tools that will allow you to collect specimens not usually obtainable by seining.

The Plankton Net

Drifting through the sea are billions of tiny plants and animals known collectively as plankton. Most forms of phytoplankton (plants) and zooplankton (animals) are microscopic in size. Plankton (from a Greek word meaning "wandering") are a basic link in the marine food chain and include transparent arrow-worms, diatoms, copepods, and the free-floating young of snails and clams. Because of their small size, plankton must be strained from the water in a finely-woven fabric. Your plankton net will be made from the leg of a nylon stocking. You'll also need a needle and strong thread, a wire coathanger, a plastic medicine vial, a large metal washer, and some stout cord.

Open the coathanger with pliers and form it into a circle about ten inches across. Overlap the ends and wrap them with fine wire, cord, or electrical tape. (See illustration.)

Slip the large, open end of the stocking inside the wire ring. Fold the edge of the stocking over the outside of the ring so that the stocking material overlaps itself with the ring inside.

Sew the ring securely within the stocking with needle and thread. Your stitches should encircle the wire. Keep the stitches tight and close together.

Snip a small hole in the toe of the stocking, just big enough to insert your plastic medicine vial. Tie it firmly in place with several wrappings of cord against the lip of the vial.

Cut four, 18-inch lengths of cord and tie each of them to the wire ring, evenly spaced apart. Tie the free ends to a large metal washer. (See illustration.)

Lastly, cut a six-foot length of cord and tie it to the washer, to serve as your tow line. You can tie a short piece of dowel or a stick to the end of the line as a handle.

To use the plankton net, pull it along behind you as you wade in the water. It can also be dangled into tidal currents from a pier or bridge, or towed slowly behind a boat.

The plankton will be strained from the water and will collect in the plastic vial as a thick organic, or living, soup.

Transport your plankton in a one-quart glass jar with a tight-fitting lid. Pour several vials of captured plankton into the jar and add a small amount of sea water.

You will need a powerful hand lens or a microscope to clearly see and study the rich variety of life that makes up plankton.

The Dip Net

This easy-to-make collecting device will capture any specimens capable of being caught in a seine net. However, the long-handled dip net can reach into tight spots not accessible to the seine. Use it in a boat to land hooked fish or snatch up turtles. From a pier or a stone jetty, you can reach out and snare starfish, crabs, or jellyfish. The net is excellent for work in marshy backwaters and tidal pools.

To construct your dip net you'll need these materials: a piece of cheesecloth (at least 36 inches square), a wire coathanger, a broomstick, white glue or household cement (epoxy), and a needle and strong thread.

Open the coathanger with pliers and form it into a ten-inch circle. Bend the last three inches of each end of the wire at a right angle, away from the circle, as shown in the illustration.

Drill a ¼" hole in the end of the broomstick to a depth of three inches. (If the broomstick has a threaded end, cut this off first.)

Insert the bent ends of the net's circular wire frame into the hole in the broomstick. The natural springiness of the wire will keep it in place.

Squeeze white glue or epoxy into the hole, completely filling it, and allow it to dry for several hours.

Cut a 36" circle from the cheesecloth. Form it into a basket shape and sew it with closely-spaced, tight stitches to the wire ring. You're ready to go.

The Scoop

A one-gallon plastic bleach bottle is the raw material for a handy scoop that will unearth lugworms, clam worms, mole crabs, and sand lances.

Leave the cap tightly sealed on the bottle. Place the bottle on its side with the pre-formed handle facing up. Using a sharp hobby knife, make an angled cut from the middle of the bottle towards the bottom to form a scoop, as shown in the illustration.

Use your scoop on mud flats, along the upper fringes of the surf zone, and in the shallows of the bay and salt marshes.

It's a good idea to dump your scooped soil sample onto a piece of framed window screening or into a fine-meshed kitchen strainer. You can then pour water gently over your sample to rinse away mud sediments. Your trapped organisms will be more clearly visible. Place them in a small pan of seawater to better observe their behavior.

Take care in handling any organism with which you are unfamiliar. Always consult your field guides. Few dancers can match the graceful undulations of a free-swimming clam worm. But be careful! Clam worms are predators with powerful pincing jaws that can inflict a painful bite. The jaws remain hidden, within the head, and extend outwards suddenly when the worm is disturbed.

Always remember to release your organisms when your study is complete.

And that's the scoop on using your scoop.

Plankton Nets, Dip Nets, and Scoops

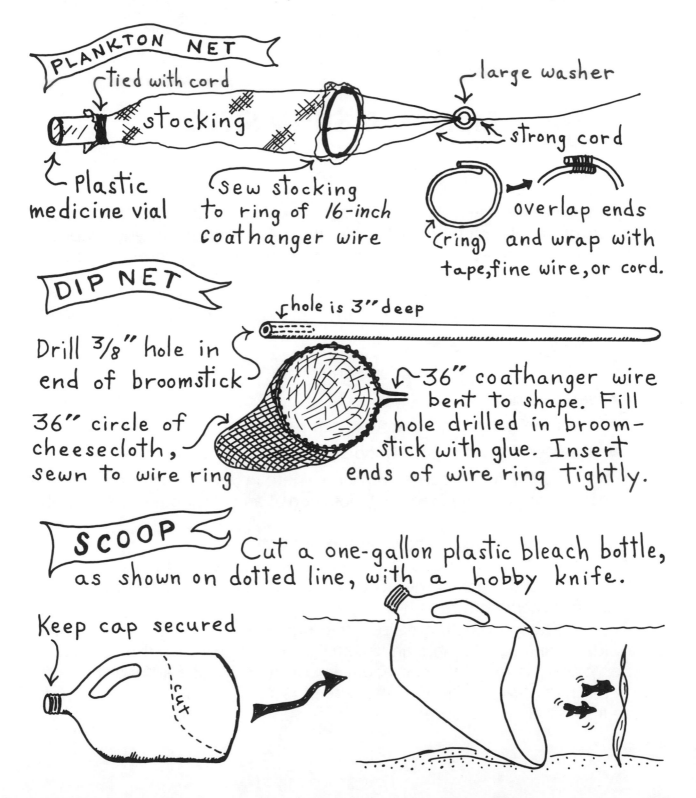

PLANKTON NET

tied with cord

stocking

large washer

strong cord

Plastic medicine vial

sew stocking to ring of 16-inch coathanger wire

(ring) overlap ends and wrap with tape, fine wire, or cord.

DIP NET

hole is 3" deep

Drill 3/8" hole in end of broomstick

36" circle of cheesecloth, sewn to wire ring

36" coathanger wire bent to shape. Fill hole drilled in broomstick with glue. Insert ends of wire ring tightly.

SCOOP Cut a one-gallon plastic bleach bottle, as shown on dotted line, with a hobby knife.

Keep cap secured

cut

51

MUD AND SAND SIEVE

This simple device is easy and fun to build. It can be added to your collection of animal-trapping tools. You will use it along with your scoop to expose marine organisms living in the soft substrates (mud or sand) along the shores. The word substrate refers to the base on or in which an organism lives, such as mud, sand, or rock.

To build the sieve you'll need:

- package of ½" carpet tacks
- 26" by 26" piece of window screening
- serrated nails
- common nails (eight-penny or ten-penny sizes)
- 4 pieces of two-by-four wood stock, each 24" long

You'll probably find these items somewhere in your garage or basement, but they are easily and inexpensively obtained at any hardware shop or lumber yard.

Assemble the sieve as shown in the illustration.

To construct the frame, first drive one or two serrated nails across the tops of the joints at each corner. Then drive two common nails into the ends of each joint for added strength.

Before tacking down the screen, fold under the edges about a half-inch on all sides. This will eliminate any scratchy wire ends. Attach the screen with a series of carpet tacks spaced about every three inches around the entire perimeter of the frame. Be sure the screen is centered and aligned properly on the frame before tacking.

To use the sieve, dig deeply into the sand along the surf zone of the ocean beach or into the soil at the water's edge at the bayside. You may use your scoop, a shovel, or small pitchfork. Dump the soil onto the sieve and gently rinse the soil away with a bucket of water, a little at a time. Probe the soil with your fingertips and keep a sharp eye out for any movement.

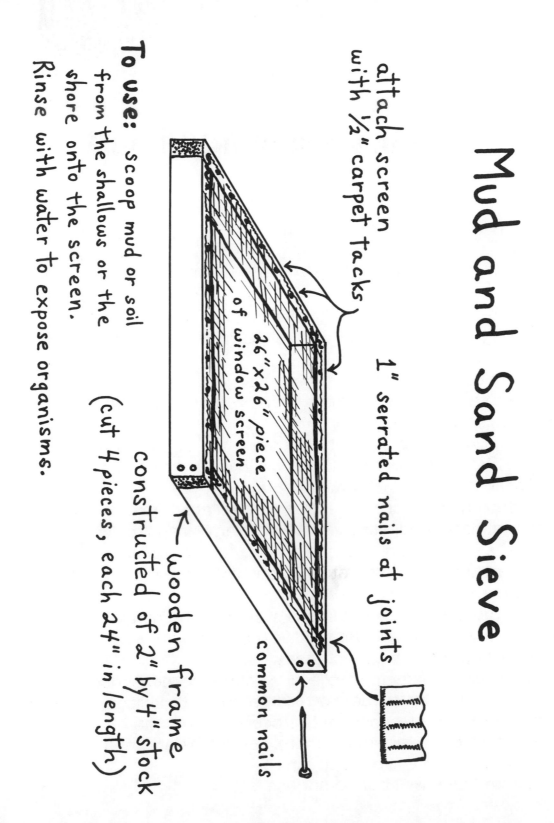

Mud and Sand Sieve

attach screen with ½" carpet tacks

1" serrated nails at joints

26"x26" piece of window screen

common nails

wooden frame constructed of 2" by 4" stock (cut 4 pieces, each 24" in length)

To use: Scoop mud or soil from the shallows or the shore onto the screen. Rinse with water to expose organisms.

THE MARINE AQUARIUM

Most people believe the aquarium is a true microcosm, or world in miniature, of a natural environment. This is not so. Sea water is a "living" substance that contains numerous micro-organisms and it is in constant interaction with the biosphere. The marine aquarium is an artificial, closed system and long-term maintenance requires elaborate filtering and aeration systems. The removal of nitrogenous animal wastes, normally controlled by marine plants, cannot be successfully duplicated.

In spite of these difficulties, it is possible to set up and maintain a working system for several months. Your efforts will be rewarded with long hours of exciting observation and study.

Keep in mind, we are not discussing the set-up of a pet store type of tropical fish tank. Rather, the set-up will involve the collection and transportation of local specimens in natural sea water.

A natural marine, or salt water, aquarium at home or in the classroom will provide a rare and fascinating view of an unfamiliar and misunderstood environment. The salt water aquarium is a powerful tool to arouse curiosity and increase awareness of the delicate relationships that exist among the inhabitants of a marine eco-system.

There are many excellent books available on aquariums. They can provide detailed information to answer specific questions. However, the following basic ideas are adequate to insure success.

Set up your tank before collecting your specimens. Use an all glass tank, as those with metal frames or with plastic (Plexiglass) walls emit small amounts of toxic (poisonous) substances into the water.

Salt water species demand room. Use a tank of twenty gallon capacity or larger. I prefer a thirty-five gallon tank.

Wash the tank well but do not use soap.

Marine fish also consume a great deal of oxygen. Your air pump must run continuously, twenty-four hours a day. A small vibrator pump will deliver enough air to operate a corner filter and an airstone. Purchase an inexpensive "T" fitting at a pet shop and set up your air lines.

Natural sea water contains many bacteria and pollutants which cause it to deteriorate rather quickly. You can slow down this process and help to stabilize your set-up by mixing a half tank of artificial sea water using a commercially prepared product. *Instant Ocean* sea salts are a popular brand, found in most aquarium supply shops. Or, you can order them from the Carolina Biological Supply Co., Burlington, N.C. 27215. Fill the remainder of the tank with natural sea water, used to transport your specimens. (For ideas on specimen collecting, see the preceding chapters on seining and hand-made collection devices.)

Let the filter and aeration system run for forty-eight hours.

Collect your specimens (in moderation, please) along with enough marine soil or gravel to cover the tank bottom to a two inch depth. Include plenty of various algaes, as they will provide both a food source and a protective cover in which some of the smaller organisms may hide. Plastic five-gallon pails with snap-on lids are best suited for the tasks of collection and transportation of water and animals.

Transfer your specimens and sea water immediately into your tank. Most of your animals will survive but some, invariably, will die of shock, unable to adjust to the dramatic change. Be prepared for this and quickly remove dead animals from the tank. (Decaying animals produce ammoniated wastes which are harmful to the surviving animals.)

Your aquarium will require some care and attention, but the following tasks do not involve great sums of time and effort:

- Set up a feeding schedule, (every other day,) and avoid overfeeding.
- Remove dead animals at once.
- Remove any uneaten food promptly.
- Clean the filter as needed.
- Add water as needed to replace any lost by evaporation. Use only fresh water, distilled or aged for a day. (Salt is not lost through evaporation.)
- Avoid overpopulation, direct sunlight, and sudden changes in temperature.
- Change one third of the aquarium water on a monthly basis. This will reduce ammonia concentrations in the water and will replace important trace elements which have been consumed by fish and plants.

Try for an interesting variety of animal forms in your tank. Can you discover the relationships that exist between predators and prey in your salt water community? Perhaps you could draw and label a food chain to represent your aquarium. What devices are used by your animals for defense? Do they use speed, camouflage, or do they possess defensive weapons of some kind?

Study also the methods of movement used by your animals. We call this locomotion. My own students have witnessed the throbbing rhythms of jellyfish, the slow-motion crawl of starfish, and the clattering, jerky movements of a shell-clacking, swimming scallop. Also exciting are shrimp, crabs, pipefish, and sea horses.

Occasionally add a new organism. Look for new interactions and changed behaviors in your mini-marine-environment.

And enjoy the deep sense of wonder that your marine aquarium is sure to awaken within you.

Simplified Set-up for a Marine Aquarium

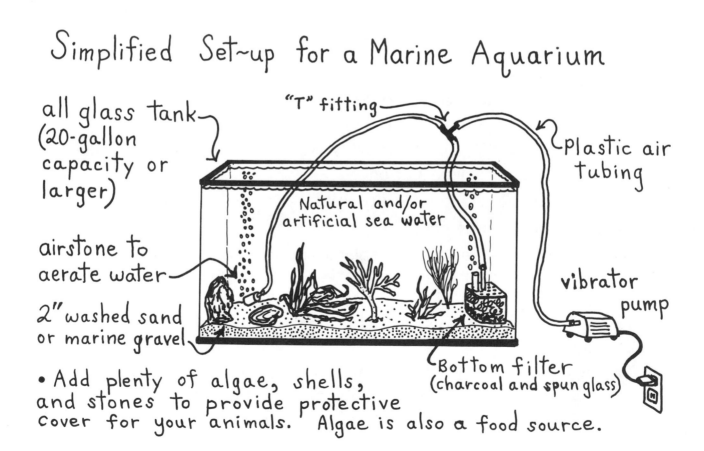

all glass tank (20-gallon capacity or larger)

"T" fitting

Plastic air tubing

airstone to aerate water

Natural and/or artificial sea water

2" washed sand or marine gravel

vibrator pump

Bottom filter (charcoal and spun glass)

• Add plenty of algae, shells, and stones to provide protective cover for your animals. Algae is also a food source.

SALT MARSH WORD SEARCH

Our coastal salt marshes and beaches are teeming with thousands of fascinating objects and life forms. But only the sharpest eyes will catch them all.

How sharp are your eyes? To find out, try the word search game on the following page. Thirty-two items can be found hidden in the grid, written horizontally, vertically, or diagonally. All words appear in straight lines, but may be written backward as well as forward.

See how many items you can pick out and circle on your own. Then, use the master list below to help you finish. If a term on the list is strange to you, why not check your field guides or an encyclopedia? Happy hunting.

Word List for the Salt Marsh Word Search

whelk	plankton	shrimp	seine
kelp	seaweed	shell	hermit crab
fox	raccoon	egret	barnacles
marsh	seagulls	swan	cordgrass
eel	lobster	peat	periwinkle
tides	muskrat	duck	mussel
fish	nursery	clam	oyster
dune	shiner	shore	mud snail

Salt Marsh Word Search

32 items related to the sea are hidden in the grid. Each will read in a straight line horizontally, vertically, or diagonally. How many can you find?

W	H	E	L	K	E	N	U	D	Q	U	B	X	O	F
S	A	P	R	E	P	A	L	U	R	N	A	S	M	H
E	W	S	C	L	A	M	G	C	E	O	R	H	S	E
I	K	V	T	P	L	A	N	K	T	O	N	O	E	R
N	W	R	E	T	S	Y	O	M	S	C	A	R	A	M
E	Y	A	X	M	R	D	C	L	B	C	C	E	G	I
N	T	O	J	E	U	V	T	E	O	A	L	O	U	T
M	A	R	S	H	R	I	M	P	L	R	E	Z	L	C
D	U	R	E	Z	D	E	E	W	A	E	S	T	L	R
G	U	S	F	E	S	H	I	N	E	R	G	W	S	A
N	F	S	S	A	R	G	D	R	O	C	M	R	A	B
H	I	C	N	E	M	U	D	S	N	A	I	L	E	N
B	S	K	P	E	L	K	N	I	W	I	R	E	P	T
S	H	E	L	L	I	J	L	M	U	S	K	R	A	T

FISH PRINTING

The next time you go fishing, how about framing your catch and mounting it on the wall? No, we're not talking about some complicated taxidermy, but a simple, direct-contact process that will produce a detailed, technically accurate art print of any fish. You can perform the activity right on the beach or at home.

The method to be described will work on shellfish such as clams and scallops, as well as the fin fishes. With a little practice, your textured prints will capture finely defined details like gill covers (operculums), scales, lateral lines, facial features, and each distinct bony ray of the various fins.

For your first attempt, try printing flat fishes like flounder and fluke, or narrow-bodied fishes like porgies. Another good idea is to try the shell of a large surf clam. (See photographs for examples.) Of course, if your fishing trip hasn't been successful, you can always purchase your fish at a seafood retailer.

You'll need the following materials: several newspapers, a 2" paint brush or brayer (small rubber printing roller), a pint of black tempera paint (other colors may also be used), and some sheets of 12" by 18" white watercolor paper, (which may be cut to smaller sizes as needed.)

To make your prints, spread open the newspapers and separate them into two piles, one for "inking" the fish with paint and the other for your contact printing. (See illustration.)

Set~up for Fish Printing

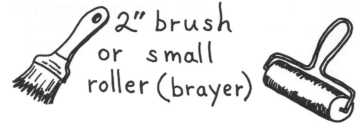
2" brush
or small
roller (brayer)

pint of
tempera
paint

BLACK

"Ink" fish on one pile; transfer
to second pile to make print

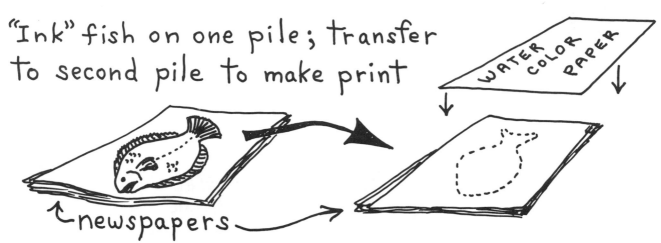

WATER COLOR PAPER

newspapers

Place the fish or shell to be printed in the center of the pile of newspapers to be used for "inking." Using a small brush or roller, spread a light even coat of tempera paint over the fish. Be sure the surface of the fish is completely covered.

Being careful not to remove any paint, slide your hand under the fish and gently transfer it to the center of the second stack of newspapers. Do not allow any paint to drip or smear on this newspaper as it will be picked up on your print.

Take a sheet of white watercolor paper and hold it centered over the fish. Slowly place it down, directly onto the "inked" fish.

With one hand and using light pressure, hold the paper in position as you carefully press the paper down over the entire fish surface with the fingers of your free hand. Do not allow the paper to slide once it has made contact with the fish or your print will be hopelessly smeared.

When you are satisfied that all parts of the fish have made contact with the paper, lift it up carefully. Drying should occur in ten minutes.

Do not expect the first print to be the best. Usually, the first print helps to remove sticky slime and excessive paint from areas that were too heavily "inked." Without adding more paint, make a second, third, and fourth print. These will be better. Each print, of course, requires a new sheet of watercolor paper. Do not repeat the "inking" process until you can no longer print a full image.

Each time you roll or brush paint onto your fish, remove the top sheets of newspaper from each pile and begin with fresh sheets. Please dispose of the used newspapers properly.

You can title your prints in hand written fashion or by using press-on lettering available at stationery or art shops. Do a little research and label your fish print in both its generic and scientific names. For example: PORGY — Stenotomus chrysops.

Of course, your prints may be displayed purely as art. But endless ideas await hobbyists and students seeking projects for art or science classes.

Beautiful booklets can be created from these prints. How about producing some personalized artistic stationery? Or using your prints to illustrate original nature poetry? You can even turn your print into an attractive science poster by labeling and explaining the function of each fin on the body of the fish. And don't overlook the fact that this procedure will also work with plants.

SURF CLAM

FLOUNDER

SALT-MEADOW GRASS SCARECROW DOLLS

How about creating something truly unique? A scarecrow doll, made in the spirit of our colonial ancestors, can be made from a grass common to the salt marshes on our coast. The grass you'll need is *Spartina patens,* more popularly known as salt-meadow grass or salt-meadow hay. It was once a valued crop of our early coastal settlers. Farmers harvested tons as winter feed and bedding for their cattle. It was even used to thatch the roofs of their homes. You'll use it to create an early American toy, a scarecrow doll.

You should have no trouble recognizing the salt-meadow grass. It is the dominant grass in most marshes. It grows in flattened patches or "cowlicks" that appear to have been trampled down. The leaves are slender, u-shaped, and average two feet in length.

Salt-meadow grass is best obtained at low tide. Since the grass generally inhabits the drier, highwater zones of the marsh, it can usually be collected without getting your feet wet. You can gather your grass from spring through fall, but during August the grass will be bearing its dark purple fruits.

To collect the grass, do not uproot the plant. Instead, use scissors to cut a heavy handful of leaves, several inches thick, close to the base of the plant.

Soak the leaves in a pan of fresh water and swish them about to remove any salt residue. Then, spread the grass out to dry on some paper towels. When dry, re-bundle the grass and trim both ends straight and even with scissors. The clutch of grass should be about ten inches long.

Separate the large clutch of grass into two smaller bundles, one bundle of one inch thickness and the other of a half-inch in thickness. The thicker bundle will be used to form the head, body, and legs. The smaller bundle will form the arms. The leaves of salt-meadow grass are flexible and easily worked to shape. You'll need some strong kite string to tie the grass into shape for the various body parts. Simply follow the illustrated steps for making these ties. Always snip excess string close to the knots.

Clothing can be made from colored construction paper or from colorful cloth scraps. If you choose to make your scarecrow's clothing from cloth, a needle and fine thread will be needed for sewing. Paper clothing can be cut from drawn patterns and pasted to fit the scarecrow. Suggested ideas are found in the illustrated instructions.

Facial details (eyes, nose, mouth) can be glued on last. Small beaded eyes can be purchased at novelty stores or the notions counter at a large department store. The nose and mouth can be made by inserting cloves into the grass and gluing them in place with white glue. Or, try cutting an oval of white paper or cloth and drawing in your facial features with a fine-tipped marking pen. Then, glue the entire face onto the doll.

A cone-shaped hat is easily made from a two-inch circle of cloth or construction paper. Black construction paper looks best. Slit the circle from the edge to the circle's center in a straight line. Overlap one cut edge onto the other to form the cone and glue the edges together. (See illustrations.) Glue the hat onto your doll's head.

As a plaything or as a showpiece, your salt-meadow grass scarecrow doll is sure to grab attention.

Beach Grass Scarecrow Doll

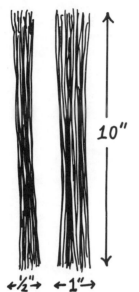

10"

←½"→ ←1"→

Fig. A

1. Obtain two clutches of salt~meadow grass as shown in figure A.

2. With string, make a tight tie around the large clutch of grass about 1 inch from the top. (fig. B)

3. Holding the head, turn the figure upside down. Fold the grass blades firmly down and around the head. Tie again to form the neck. (fig C)

4. Three inches below the neck, tie the waist. Separate the remaining grass to form two legs. Tie each leg just below the waist and at the ankles.

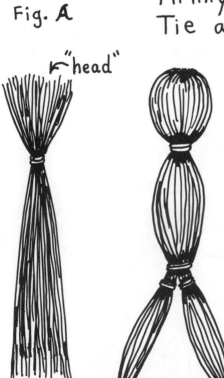

"head"

Fig. B   Fig. C

Fig. D (Arms)

ᵗtie   ᵗtie

5. To form the arms and hands of the doll, make two ties on the smaller clutch of grass, about ½" in from each end.

6. Assemble the doll by inserting the "arms" into the body. Gently separate the grass below the neck with a butter knife. Insert and center the arms, then bind by criss~crossing snugly with string as shown. (Fig E)

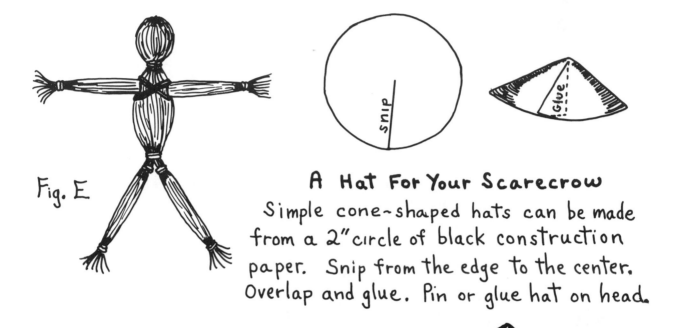

Fig. E

snip

Glue

A Hat For Your Scarecrow

Simple cone~shaped hats can be made from a 2" circle of black construction paper. Snip from the edge to the center. Overlap and glue. Pin or glue hat on head.

Plastic eyes purchased at craft shop or notions counter

Clothing: Lay completed doll upon <u>doubled</u> sheets of cloth or paper. Trace around doll leaving ¼" margin as shown by dotted lines. Pants and shirt may be made as one piece or as two. Cut out patterns.

Center doll on lower pattern and run a narrow bead of glue along edges of pattern. Place second pattern over doll and seal all seams. (If using white paper, color before gluing. Cloth patterns may be sewn.)

SAND PAINTING PROJECTS

Captivating art work can be produced with colored sands. Long ago, the Navajo Indians of our American Southwest discovered the beauty of this craft and created elaborate designs by sprinkling the colored sands onto the ground in symbolic patterns for tribal celebrations and religious rituals. Let's see how we can reproduce this art form and several others that use colored sands.

How to Dye the Sand

There are two methods to be described and both work well. In either case, you will need a good amount of clean, dry, white sand collected from the beach. Be sure it is free of any bits of dried seaweed, twigs, or other beach debris.

Method 1: If you are working alone and do not require many colors, fill a set of baby food jars about three-quarters full of sand. Using standard food colors, squirt liberal amounts of each color into each jar. Replace the lids and shake vigorously for about ten seconds. The dyed sand may be used immediately. For deeper colors, add more food coloring. Or, you may combine the basic food colors to produce other shades such as purple, orange or brown.

Method 2: This technique requires larger containers and a set of tempera paints. It is best used for large group projects or whenever a wide variety of dense colors is required. Old cookie tins work well, but you may use large bowls or deep baking pans, also. Add sand to the containers until they are three-quarters full. In separate containers, thin down the tempera paints with water to a soupy consistency. Do not mix a large amount of paint. It goes a long way. Pour the paint into the containers of sand, a little at a time, and stir until the desired color is evenly distributed throughout the sand.

Pour the sand onto several thicknesses of newspaper and spread it out to dry. This may take ten to twenty minutes. When dry, return the sand to the containers for use or storage. Tempera paints are available in pint-sized squeeze bottles and boast a wide array of colors.

Now that we have our sand dyed, here are a couple of suggestions for its use in art.

Painted Sand Pictures

You may use your dyed sand to recreate a Navajo sand painting. A reference book from your library will provide ideas for authentic symbols and designs. Scratch the symbols into the ground and fill in the areas between the lines with appropriate colors by sprinkling sand with your fingertips. This takes practice. Work slowly. Of course, your finished artwork is not permanent. It can't be picked up and displayed elsewhere.

For permanent paintings, try this. On a piece of heavy cardboard or oaktag, draw a seashore scene or Indian design in bold outline form. Decide upon colors for each section of your picture and pencil in a letter for each color; (R = red, Y = yellow, and so on.)

Using a stiff narrow brush, paint in areas of a particular color with a slightly thinned mixture of white glue and water. Work one color at a time. Be sure the glue is spread evenly over all the surface between the bold lines. Sprinkle the colored sand immediately onto the wet glue. Let it set a few moments. Shake any unglued sand back into the container and proceed with the next color.

Your finished sand painting can be framed and hung anywhere.

Layered Sand Art

Another fascinating effect is achieved by layering your sand into a deep wine glass or water goblet. Sprinkle layers of sand in varying thicknesses and color combinations until the glass is full to within a half-inch from the rim.

Use a pencil and a piece of wire to probe down into the sand along the inside edge of the glass. This will create deep "V" patterns in the colors. Remove these probes carefully. Your layered sand art can be displayed on a sunlit shelf where the colors will be brightly illuminated. Tall, round or square bottles make other interesting containers for layered sand art. Experiment for interesting results.

Sand Painting

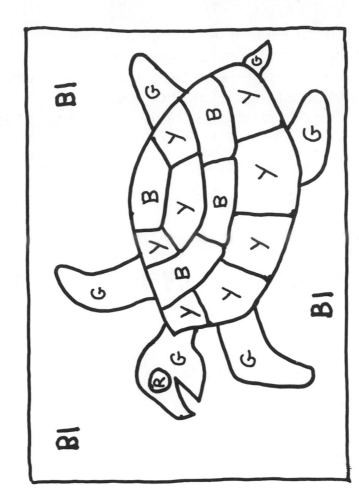

Bl   Bl

Bl   Bl

Bl = blue   R = red   G = green
Y = yellow   B = black

Layered Sand Art

BEACH PLUM JELLY AND PRESERVES

Beach plums are native wild fruits found in most dune communities along the northern east coast. The plants grow as thick low-mounded shrubs. The stiff reddish-brown branches bear numerous white blossoms from the end of April to early June. The blossoms become pink with age. The fruits ripen in the fall, from the end of September into early October.

Beach plums vary in size from as big around as a nickel to the size of a quarter. Fully ripened fruits are bluish-purple to bluish-black in color. Slightly underripe fruits may have reddish purple tinges. These may be a bit tart to eat raw, but they can be used successfully in preparing jellies and preserves.

Beach plums can most often be found on the dune slopes, either on the back face of the primary dune (landward side), or on the front face (seaward side) of the secondary dune. They can also be found growing on the crests of the dunes, as they have a natural tolerance to air-borne salt spray. The plants are often found growing in close proximity to bayberry, salt spray rose, and high bush blueberry.

Firm, tart beach plums were eaten by Native American coastal tribes and were a favorite with early colonists in pies, jellies, and preserves.

During your next walk along the beach this fall, bring along a pail and pick about 2½ quarts (about five pounds) of beach plums. Include a handful of slightly underripe fruits as they contain higher concentrations of acid and pectin. These elements are important to the jellying process. The nice thing about beach plums is that they contain enough acid and pectin in their natural state so that the addition of commercially prepared pectin is unnecessary.

Beach Plum Jelly

Pick over the fruit to remove any stems, then wash the fruits in cold water.

The making of jelly requires two cookings. The first extracts the juice from the fruit and the second cooking combines sugar and juice, causing the mixture to gel.

To prepare the juice, place about five cups of beach plums into a large wide-mouthed kettle of four quart size or larger. Use either stainless steel or enameled kettles. Mash the fruit in the kettle with a wooden masher. Try not to crush the pits as this will cause bitterness. Add a small amount of water, enough to just cover the fruit. Bring the fruit to a boil and simmer for about five minutes, stirring constantly until the fruit is disintegrated.

Pour the cooked fruit immediately into a colander, large sieve, or double thicknesses of cheesecloth over a kettle to remove the seeds and drain out the fruit puree. Allow the fruit to drip for an hour. The cheesecloth bag can be pressed gently to extract more juice, but do not overdo this, as it can cause the jelly to appear cloudy. It will not affect the taste.

71

The addition of sugar to the juice must be done carefully. Too little sugar can cause the jelly to be rubbery, while too much sugar produces thin syrupy jellies. Measure your fruit juice and add sugar in the proportion of 2/3 cup of sugar to each cup of fruit juice. Bring the juice to a boil. Add the sugar quickly while stirring slowly. Continue to stir until all the sugar is dissolved. Keep stirring the mix as it thickens. Cooking may take fifteen minutes. To test your mixture to determine the jellying point, take a cool tablespoon and dip into the boiling juice. Raise the spoon above the steam and allow the juice to run off slowly. If the last couple of drops run together in a single sheet, remove the jelly immediately from the stove. Pour the jelly directly into hot sterilized jars and let the jelly cool. Jars may be sterilized by boiling in water. Keep the jars in hot water until ready to use. After the jelly has cooled, pour melted paraffin over the jelly and seal the jars. (This is not necessary if you plan to use the jelly right away, rather than store it.)

Beach Plum Preserves

Unlike jellies, which require two cookings, the making of preserves is done with only one cooking. Wash and pick off any stems from five cups of beach plums. Place the plums in a large kettle with four cups of sugar and one cup of water. Heat the ingredients *slowly* until the mixture comes to a boil. As mixture heats, stir continually until the sugar has completely dissolved.

At this point, cook the mixture rapidly and test it for readiness to gel using the spoon sheeting method described for beach plum jelly. The cooking may take fifteen minutes. Pour it through a colander to remove seeds and seal the preserves in jars or use it immediately.

There are ready-made items which can be purchased to aid you in jelly making. These include jelly bags and stands for draining off juice and special thermometers that can be used in place of the sheeting test to determine the gelation point of the heated mixture. If your first batch isn't quite right, try again, adding less sugar to make the jelly firmer, or more sugar to thin the jelly. A rich, thick, sweet beach plum jelly or preserve is well worth the effort. If you're careful, you won't end up in a "jam."

SALT-SPRAY ROSE-HIP JELLY

Salt-Spray Rose (Rosa rugosa)

The Salt-Spray Rose (Rosa rugosa) is common to the dunes of the Middle Atlantic and Northern Atlantic coasts. It grows as dense shrubbery on both the crest and back face (landward side) of the primary dune and is often found on the fore face (seaward side) of the secondary dune. It crowds in, side by side, with beach plums.

The plant provides texture and color to the sandy coastal landscape with its dark green leaflets and numerous bursts of rosy-white flowers that bloom throughout the summer and up until the first frost.

As fall approaches, the fruits, or rose hips, swell and ripen to a vivid red. Rose hips are used commercially in the production of natural vitamin C tablets. But they provide the makings for a delicious, nutritious, and distinctive jelly, too.

It would be a fine idea to gather your rose hips along with your beach plums, as they ripen at the same time (from mid-September through early October). Keep the rose hips in a separate container. When picking rose hips, wear a pair of light gloves to protect yourself from the many small, but sharp, thorns which cover the stems of the plant.

The making of rose hip jelly requires some different procedures as compared to preparing beach plum preserves. Simply, rose hips do not contain enough natural pectin and acid for jellying, so apple juice and commercially-prepared powdered pectin will be needed. Let's proceed.

Where to Find Rose Hips and Beach Plums

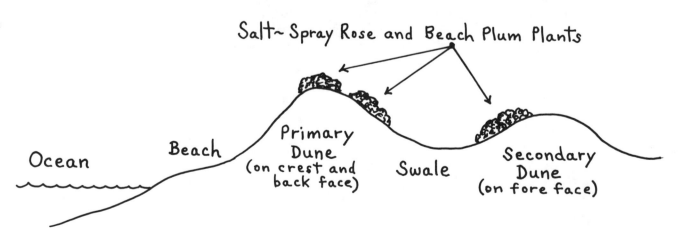

Salt~Spray Rose and Beach Plum Plants

Ocean Beach Primary Dune (on crest and back face) Swale Secondary Dune (on fore face)

After collecting sufficient fruit, (several quarts will do nicely,) pick off all the stem ends and dried sepals from the hips. Wash the fruit in cold water. Measure out the rose hips in a measuring cup and pour them into a large, open steel or enameled kettle. Add two cups of cold water for each cup of fruit. Bring the water to a boil and simmer the hips for twelve to fifteen minutes or until they are soft.

Being careful not to crush the seeds of the fruit, mash the hips with a wooden masher. (If you wish to spice up your jelly, a half-teaspoon of cinnamon or mace may be added at this time.) Continue to boil the mixture for another ten minutes, then remove the kettle from the heat and let it stand undisturbed for twenty-four hours.

Now, strain the juice through a double layer of cheesecloth or a cloth jelly bag.

Measure out your volume of juice in cups. For *each* 2½ cups of rose hip juice you must add one box of commercially-prepared pectin *and* one cup of clear apple juice. Stir gently until all the pectin has dissolved and then heat the mixture to a full boil. Keep the mix simmering and stir in 4½ cups of sugar to each 2½ cups of juice you had prepared. Cook the mixture for about five minutes more or until the thickening jelly will run off a large spoon in sheets. Stir occasionally as the jelly is cooking. At this point, remove the jelly from the heat.

As the jelly boiled and thickened, a foam may have formed. Skim this off before pouring the jelly into heated sterile glasses. Allow the jelly to cool slightly before sealing the glasses with melted paraffin. If the jelly is to be used quickly, sealing is not necessary.

Rose hip jelly is a delightful and delicious way of ensuring a healthy dose of vitamin C. Rose hips are actually richer in vitamin C than oranges. "Hip, hip," hooray! Enjoy!

WAMPUM WONDERS

What is wampum? Most people recognize the word and simply state, "Oh, that's Indian money made from shells." But wampum is a great deal more, and such a simple definition ignores the social and historical importance of wampum to the coastal tribes of the North Atlantic region, more specifically the New England tribes such as Algonkians.

It is true that wampum was made from shell, a natural resource given up by the sea. The Indians used the shell of conch and whelk to produce pinkish or tan colored beads of wampum, and the shell of the quahog, or hard-shell clam, to produce the more valuable purple beads. The lighter colors were known as wompi and the darker colors were known as sacki. The work that went into creating the beads was part of the system of value. The beads were strung into elaborate belts, gorgets (neckware), and often found their way into clothing.

Wampum became more widely used as currency, or money, only after the arrival of the white man. Previous to that time wampum was worn as ornaments and became the symbol of wealth and position within the tribe. The possession of wampum was also believed to assure acceptance into the "Happy Hunting Ground" upon death.

Many treaties were sealed by the exchange of wampum belts. The symbolic designs created in the wampum beadwork communicated ideas and was therefore a substitute for formal writing. The wearing of wampum was also significant in tribal ceremonies and wampum belts were even given up by tribal offenders as payment for their crimes.

Shells Used in Making Wampum Beads

Quahog or Hard-Shell Clam
(Mercenaria mercenaria)
4~5 inches (10~12.5 cm)

Knobbed Whelk
(Busycon caricum)
7~9 inches (18~23 cm)

Let's re-live a bit of history by discovering the natural beauty of the shells used in producing wampum. A walk along the beach through the surf and tide zones will usually turn up shell fragments of irregular shape and size. These make fine raw materials for your wampum. Look for pieces whose edges have been polished smooth by the action of waves and sand. The interior faces of the shells contain the dramatic colors you are seeking. The purpled fragments of clam shells are more often found than conch or whelk. Most often, one finds a partial whelk shell of deep tan whorls and you will have to break off pieces and smooth the edges with a file or sandpaper. This activity does not recommend creating beads from the shell material as it requires sharp, specialized tools. Rather, we will discuss polishing techniques to turn your shell fragments into attractive collector pieces for display in a fancy glass jar or to be set into jewelry. Inexpensive earrings and necklaces with blank settings can be purchased at many craft shops. Simply attach your wampum pieces with a drop of epoxy.

The shells you find on the beach may already appear attractive but most will have a cloudy luster. You can brush or spray the shell surface with a thin coat of clear, glossy polyurethane, available at any paint supply or hardware shop. A better idea is to polish the shells with a powdered porcelain cleanser. Sprinkle the cleanser liberally onto a piece of wet chamois cloth and work the shell back and forth with moderate pressure for several minutes, or until you are satisfied with the finish on the shell. Then rinse.

The finest results are gotten using techniques employed by professionals who work with gems and minerals. Gemstones are polished by using powdered abrasives of increasingly finer grades. This process enhances and deepens the natural colors and puts a gleaming shine on the surface. The method also works wonders on hard shell material.

Professional polishing compounds are available at reasonable prices. Look in your phone directory for a local lapidary. These shops specialize in artwork and jewelry created from stone, gems, crystalline minerals, and shells. If there are no lapidaries in your area, you can write to the following company:

LORTONE,™ inc.
Seattle, WA 98107

Ask for information and mail order prices on their set of four abrasives called "Lortone Tumbling Charges." The four canisters contain coarse, medium, and fine abrasives, and a finishing polish.
You can also contact:

Ecolin Co., Inc.
Lighthouse Landing
14 East Broadway
Port Jefferson, NY 11777
(516) 473-1117

I suggest you call and speak directly to the owners, Russ and Linda Baker. They are knowledgeable and extremely helpful, and carry the products mentioned above. They also stock an inexpensive hand-polishing kit called the Stroker Hand Cabbing System which is also manufactured by LORTONE,™ inc. If you are ever in the area, make a point to visit this most beautiful lapidary. It will be a memorable experience, as the shop is crowded with unique and beautiful product displays which include crystals, fossils, gems, minerals, and shells.

Whichever method you choose to use in preparing your wampum, remember it will be given greater value by the amount of work you put into it. Beautiful wampum jewelry can be seen and purchased at:

Port of Ivory
126 Main Street
Port Jefferson, NY 11777
(516) 928-5434

Call directly and speak to the proprietor and resident artist, Bernard Boriosi, for information.

Most importantly, whether you choose to simply collect wampum chips in a glass jar for display, or to produce finely polished jewelry pieces, do get to the beach and discover the beauty of this historic resource from the sea....Wampum.

SEAWATER SALINITY ACTIVITIES

All salt water is not the same. The salinity, or degree of saltiness, of water can vary greatly dependent upon the conditions of the environment. The salt content of seawater is measured by scientists in parts per thousand or ppt. However, you needn't get this technical to observe differences.

To start your experiments, visit several areas and collect water samples in quart-sized jars. For example, you might collect ocean water directly from the ocean beach, a second sample from a bay, third from a tidal pool, and perhaps another from an estuary. (An estuary is formed at the mouth of a river as it runs into the sea.) The salinity of estuaries undergoes great changes as it is affected by the surge of incoming tides. The animals and plants living in this environment are quite special in that they have the ability to tolerate these dramatic changes. At low tide, the fresh-water runoff may bring the salinity down to only 5 parts per thousand while at high tide the salinity may rise to 20 parts per thousand.

The salinity even in the open ocean is not equal. Warmer tropical waters contain more dissolved salt than cooler northern waters. It can vary from 30 to 35 parts per thousand. In addition, water samples taken from the surface of the sea after a heavy rainfall may contain less salt than deeper water layers. The sample you collect from a shallow bay or a tidal pool during the summer may have a high salt content due to evaporation of water into the atmosphere. Remember, only the water evaporates, not the salt.

As you collect your samples, label each one as to the exact location it was found. You might also note important details that could affect the salt content such as a morning rainstorm, a nearby freshwater stream, or the fact that it is high or low tide. A typical label might look like this:

```
┌─────────────────────────────────────────────────┐
│                                                   │
│   Water Sample from Long Island Sound             │
│   Date Collected: 4/2/85      Time: 9:35 a.m.     │
│   Sample taken at low tide from shoreline.        │
│   Freshwater creek 100 yards west.                │
│                                                   │
└─────────────────────────────────────────────────┘
```

The more information you record, the better you can determine the reasons for the differences in your water samples. You might even wish to record the water temperature of each sampled area.

Take your samples home. The first test is the taste test. Believe it or not, some or us were born with highly sensitive taste buds. You may be able to taste the very slight differences in saltiness from one sample to another. With your fingertip, place a drop of one sample on your tongue and taste the saltiness. Try to remember it. Wipe or rinse your mouth and try the next sample. Does it taste more salty? Less salty? See if you can arrange the samples from most salty to least salty. Write your ideas down before beginning the next test.

For the next test you will need four shallow pans of equal size. Use aluminum pie plates. Carefully measure equal amounts of each sample and pour them into separate pie plates. Label the plates so as not to confuse the samples. Place the pie pans in a warm, sunny spot and leave them undisturbed for several days until all the water has evaporated and only salt crystals remain.

Using your naked eye, can you detect visible differences in the amounts of salt that had been dissolved in each sample? See if your results agree with your taste test.

If you have difficulty determining differences in salt amounts, take a small stiff paint brush (half-inch) and gently brush the salt from each pan into neat single piles. This may make the amounts more evident.

For a final and most accurate test you will need a scale capable of measuring in grams. Perhaps your classroom or science room has one available. (Many schools have scales that measure as fine as a tenth of a gram.) Carefully weigh each pile of salt crystals and use this information to confirm or disprove the results of your previous tests.

Most importantly, remember that salinity is *never* constant in any place. It changes with currents, tides, temperatures, and seasons, and it is affected by rainstorms, rivers, and the influences of man on the environment.

As a final suggestion, try to list the forms of sea life found in each area you test, especially shellfish like clams, oysters, and snails. Which forms like or tolerate saltier water?

SEASHORE WORD POEMS

You can express your impressions and emotions about the ocean beach in a word poem. These poetic forms need not rhyme. Simply pick a theme word about the beach, write it vertically as shown below, and allow each letter of the word to become the opening letter of each line.

As you write, create strong images for your theme word. Use powerful verbs and adjectives. Make comparisons using similes and metaphors. Here are some examples:

M *ud slurps and sucks*

A *ll about my bare feet*

R *eeds dance lightly in the breeze*

S *tiff cordgrass stands in crackled heaps*

H *erons skim silently on wide white wings*

W *ild...like an*

A *ngry animal*

V *iciously*

E *ating away the shore*

Now it's your turn! How about a word poem for OCEAN, SHARK, SANDS, BEACH, TIDES, or ALGAE? Or, try a few words of your own.

_____

_____

_____

_____

_____

_____

_____

_____

_____

_____

_____

_____

_____

_____

_____

_____

_____

_____

MOCK FOSSIL and SHELL JEWELRY

People have adorned their bodies with materials of nature for thousands of years. Items commonly used included bones, feathers, stones and shells. You can design and produce your own line of beautifully primitive amulets, bracelets and pendants by following the suggestions for making mock (imitation) fossils and for stringing interesting shells.

Mock Fossil Jewelry

Occasionally you may discover an authentic fossil on the beach, formed under pressure thousands or millions of years ago, but realistic replicas can be made with earthen clay as used in making pottery. Natural clay may be found locally in your area. If so, you might wish to dig and collect your own material. But clay is inexpensively purchased at ceramic supply shops and is also found in most school art rooms. The clay is most often gray or reddish brown in color. It must be kept moist and should be wrapped in plastic until it is to be used.

To make your fossils, form the clay into flat slabs of 1/4" to 3/8" thickness. Do this by hand or by rolling out the clay between two wooden rulers as shown.

Rolling Clay into Slabs for Mock Fossils

Keep the clay moist by sprinkling it with water. This will prevent the roller from sticking to the clay and tearing it.

Into the flattened clay, firmly press a small starfish, shell or leaf. Remove it carefully to leave a sharply defined impression. Trim any excess clay with a butter knife. You may shape the clay bordering your fossil into any interesting shape if you plan to use it as neckwear. Try a teardrop, oval, circle or triangle.

At the top of your fossil pendant, form a small neat hole by twisting a pencil point through the clay from both the front and the back. Measure a piece of yarn or leather lacing large enough to fit loosely over your head. This will be tied through the hole *after* your fossil has been fired in a kiln. (See photos for examples.)

With your mock fossil complete, allow the clay to air dry and harden for two or three days. In this state it is brittle and easily broken. It must be kiln-fired for lasting strength. If you do not have access to a kiln in a school art room, a local pottery or ceramic shop will fire your fossils for a modest fee. In fact, many shops will perform the service for free as a good will gesture.

Shell Jewelry

Shell bracelets and necklaces are easily made by stringing groups of carefully selected shells onto heavy thread. Delicate jingle shells (Anomia simplex) produce beautiful results with their translucent, pastel colors of white, orange, yellow and pink. Jingle shells received their name from the charming tinkling sound the shells make as they strike against one another on the shore.

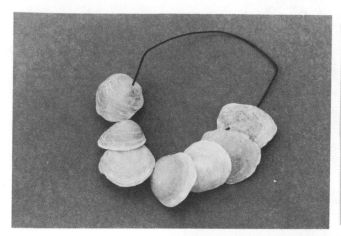

You may also use scallop or tiny clam shells, all readily available on the lower beach. Take the time to hunt for perfect shells.

At the crest of each shell, tap a tiny hole with a small nail and tack hammer. If you wish to protect and highlight the surface of your shell jewelry, spray them lightly with varnish or lacquer.

Pass a length of heavy button thread through the hole in each shell. Knot the ends to form a loop of appropriate size for a bracelet or a necklace.

Often, you may find tiny surf clam shells with pre-drilled holes ready for stringing. Your silent partner in preparing your shells for craft work is a predator of shellfish known as the moon snail (Polinices heros.) This animal plows through the sand with its oversized muscular foot until it happens upon a clam. Wrapping its foot about the shell, the moon snail begins the slow process of drilling into the clam with a rasp-like organ called the radula, producing a perfectly round, countersunk hole. It then inserts its proboscis into the hole and slowly devours the clam. The holes drilled by the moonsnail are usually on the crest of the victim's shell, just perfect for stringing on necklaces.

Inexpensive jewelry chain can be purchased as a more appealing substitute for button cord. It can add a professional quality to your finished work. See the photo for an example of a jingle shell bracelet made by children.

Moon Snail and Surf Clam

Surf Clam
(Spisula solidissima)

Hole drilled by rasp-like
radula of a moon snail

Moon Snail (Polinices heros)

BIBLIOGRAPHY

Amos, William H. *Life of the Seashore*.
New York: McGraw Hill, 1966.

The Audobon Society Book of Marine Wildlife.
New York: Harry Abrams, 1980.

Bascom, Willard. *Waves and Beaches*.
Garden City, N.Y.: Anchor Books, Doubleday, 1980.

Berrill, N.J. *The Living Tide*.
New York: Dodd Mead, 1953.

Berrill, N.J. and Jacquelyn Berrill. *One Thousand and One Questions Answered About the Seashore*.
New York: Dover Publications, 1976.

Carson, Rachel. *The Edge of the Sea*.
Boston: Houghton Mifflin Co., 1979.

Crowder, William. *Seashore Life Between the Tides*.
New York: Dover Publications, 1975.

Dawson, E. Yale. *Marine Botany, An Introduction*.
New York: Holt, Rinehart & Winston, 1966.

Edey, Maitland A. and the Editors of Time-Life Books. *The Northeast Coast*.
New York: Time-Life Books, 1972.

Gosner, Kenneth L. *A Field Guide to the Atlantic Seashore*.
Boston: Houghton Mifflin Co., 1979.

Hay, John. *The Great Beach*.
New York: W.W. Norton & Co., 1980.

Kinsbury, J.M. *Seaweeds*.
Massachusetts: The Chatham Press Inc., 1969.

Kopper, P. *The Wild Edge: Life and Lore of the Great Atlantic Beaches*.
Times Books, 1979.

MacGinitie, G.E., and Nettie MacGinitie. *Natural History of Marine Animals 2nd Edition*.
New York: McGraw Hill, 1968.

McClane, A.J. *McClane's Field Guide to Saltwater Fishes of North America*.
New York: Holt, Rinehart & Winston, 1978.

Miner, R.W. *Field Book of Seashore Life*.
New York: G.P. Putnam's Sons, 1950.

Petry, Loren C. and Marcia G. Norman. *A Beachcomber's Botany*.
Chatham: The Chatham Conservation Foundation, Inc., 1968.

Sterling, Dorothy. *The Outer Lands*.
New York: W.W. Norton & Co., Inc., 1978.

Teal, J. and M. *Life and Death of the Salt Marsh*.
New York: Little, Brown and Company, 1969.

Ursin, Michael J. *A Guide to Fishes of the Temperate Atlantic Coast*.
New York: E.P. Dutton, 1977.